Mapping Patterns of World History

Volume 2: Since 1450

Stephen Morillo
Wabash College

NEW YORK   OXFORD
OXFORD UNIVERSITY PRESS

Oxford University Press, Inc., publishes works that further Oxford University's objective of excellence in research, scholarship, and education.

Oxford New York
Auckland Cape Town Dar es Salaam Hong Kong Karachi
Kuala Lumpur Madrid Melbourne Mexico City Nairobi
New Delhi Shanghai Taipei Toronto

With offices in
Argentina Austria Brazil Chile Czech Republic France Greece
Guatemala Hungary Italy Japan Poland Portugal Singapore
South Korea Switzerland Thailand Turkey Ukraine Vietnam

For titles covered by Section 112 of the US Higher Education Opportunity Act,
please visit www.oup.com/us/he for the latest information about
pricing and alternate formats.

Published 2012 by Oxford University Press, Inc.
198 Madison Avenue, New York, New York 10016
http://www.oup.com

Oxford is a registered trademark of Oxford University Press

ISBN 978-0-19-985639-8
Printing number: 9 8 7 6 5 4 3
Printed in the United States of America
on acid-free paper

Table of Contents

Industrial Imperialism

Part 6: Adaptations to Modernity Across the Globe   **36**

1900–Present

World War I and Political Upheaval

The Great Depression and World War II

The Cold War and Decolonization

Humans and the Environment

Economics and Politics

One Changing World

Mapping Patterns of
World History

Introduction

There are many ways to tell a story about world history. Textbooks offer narratives, literal stories crafted by a modern historian or team of historians. Collections of primary sources present a mosaic of stories, often interspersed with pictures of artwork and other physical objects, drawn from the past. This sort of mosaic allows readers to take a more active role in constructing an overarching story — they recreate something of the process professional historians use to construct their narratives. Narratives and source-books are often excellent at conveying political, social, and cultural developments in particular societies, partly because almost all sources, written or visual (or even archaeological) come from single societies, with travel narratives forming a rare and valuable exception.

This book takes a different approach to telling a story about world history: it presents the world through a series of maps. Maps are not necessarily a better or worse medium for telling a global story. They are simply a different way, a way with its own advantages and disadvantages. Maps can usually convey much less detail about the political and cultural details of particular societies than narratives and primary sources can. In addition, maps that adopt a "single society" approach — the traditional sort of map of a politically defined country's political boundaries and centers of power — sometimes don't add much. They not only reinforce the sort of "nationalist" perspective narratives can lead to, but can give a false sense of the independence, coherence, and isolation of such entities.

This book attempts to take advantage of the strengths of maps to tell a different sort of story. Maps can reveal connections, by tracing the network connections — of trade, migration, and cultural exchange — and geographic contexts of individual societies. This is valuable because the tension between individual societies, often defined politically, and broader networks, defined economically, socially, and culturally, is arguably one of the central dynamics of world historical development. Maps can also act as snapshots of social history, conveying in dramatic visual terms the aggregate social developments related to demographic and economic growth or change. Like the activities of networks, such deep social trends often do not show up clearly in political narratives or the literary sources generated by social elites. Maps can thus uncover neglected layers of social history. Finally, maps are perhaps the best medium for conveying the trans-regional and even global nature of many such deep processes, from the early emergence of networks of trade through the effect of industrialization on world-wide communications to the impact of global warming on the entire planet.

Such deep processes underlie the organizational scheme of this book. There have been three big eras of human history in terms of patterns of human subsistence and population. The first took off with the emergence in our species of our capacities for symbolic thought, communication, and culture. This propelled our hunting and gathering ancestors across the globe. The invention of agriculture initiated a new wave of population growth and created the agrarian world shown in the second part of the book. Finally, industrialization began reshaping the world once more through impacts still playing themselves out today.

So welcome to a global story through maps — not a replacement for other stories, but a complementary look, another perspective on a story too vast and rich to be told in just one way.

Stephen Morillo
Wabash College

Interactions Across the Globe

PART FOUR

1450 – 1750

As the regional traditions represented in Part 3 developed and spread, they came into increasing connection with each other through expanding and strengthening network connections. Such contacts ranged from heightened military competition to growing economic exchanges, and always involved cultural encounters. And sometimes they spawned unintended consequences, such as the transmission of the Black Death across the major Eurasian trade routes. By the 1490s, the growth of global network connections began to have serious transformative effects on global patterns of exchange.

The European voyages of exploration, by linking the long-established Eurasian and Indian Ocean trade systems to the peoples and resources of previously isolated regions, especially the Americas, created a truly global network of economic and cultural exchange. The period from 1500 to 1750 then saw the agrarian or pre-industrial world reach new levels of maturity and sophistication economically, politically, and culturally.

Maps

The Global Network

The global network carried flows of goods and peoples (as well as diseases and ideas) that created new systems and reinforced old ones.

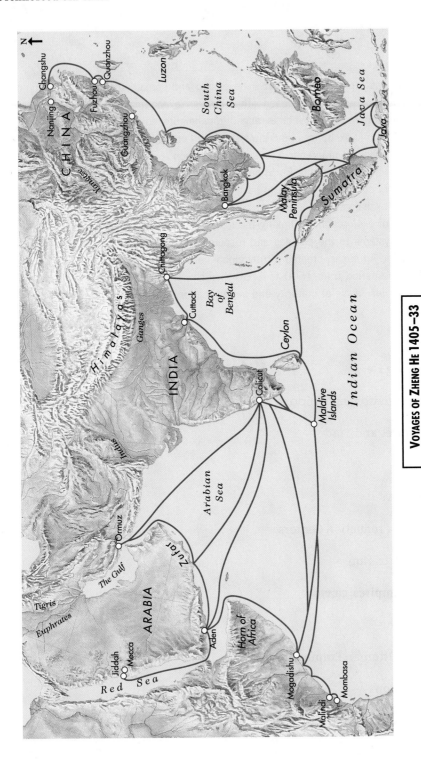

MAP 4.1 **Voyages of Zheng He.** The voyages of the early Ming Treasure Fleets, led by Admiral Zheng He, asserted Chinese centrality in the vibrant trade circuits of the South China Sea and Indian Ocean.

VOYAGES OF ZHENG HE 1405–33
—— Routes of ships from Zheng He's fleet

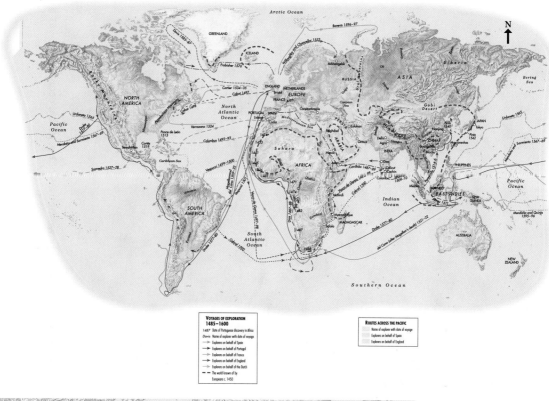

VOYAGES OF EXPLORATION
1485–1600

1487   Date of Portuguese discovery in Africa
Davis   Name of explorer with date of voyage
→   Explorers on behalf of Spain
→   Explorers on behalf of Portugal
→   Explorers on behalf of France
→   Explorers on behalf of England
→   Explorers on behalf of the Dutch
– – –   The world known of by
          Europeans c. 1450

ROUTES ACROSS THE PACIFIC

    Name of explorer with date of voyage
    Explorers on behalf of Spain
    Explorers on behalf of England

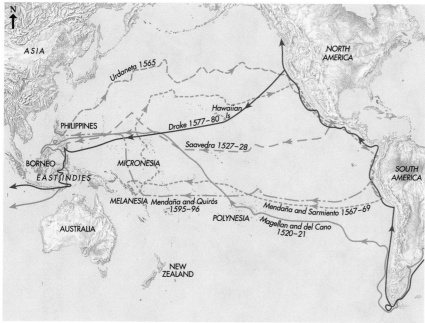

ROUTES ACROSS THE PACIFIC

Drake   Name of explorer with date of voyage
→   Explorers on behalf of Spain
→   Explorers on behalf of England

MAP 4.2 **Voyages of Exploration, 1485-1600.** The most significant expansion of the global network of exchange came with European mastery of the circular wind patterns of the Atlantic and Pacific Oceans.

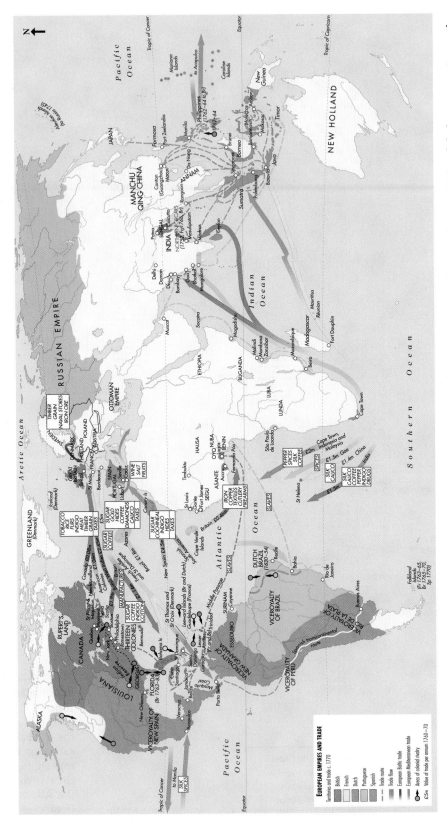

MAP 4.3 **European Empires and Trade.** Although China and India remained the great economic powerhouses of the global economy, it was the new connections forged by European merchants, adventurers, and colonists that reshaped the patterns of global trade.

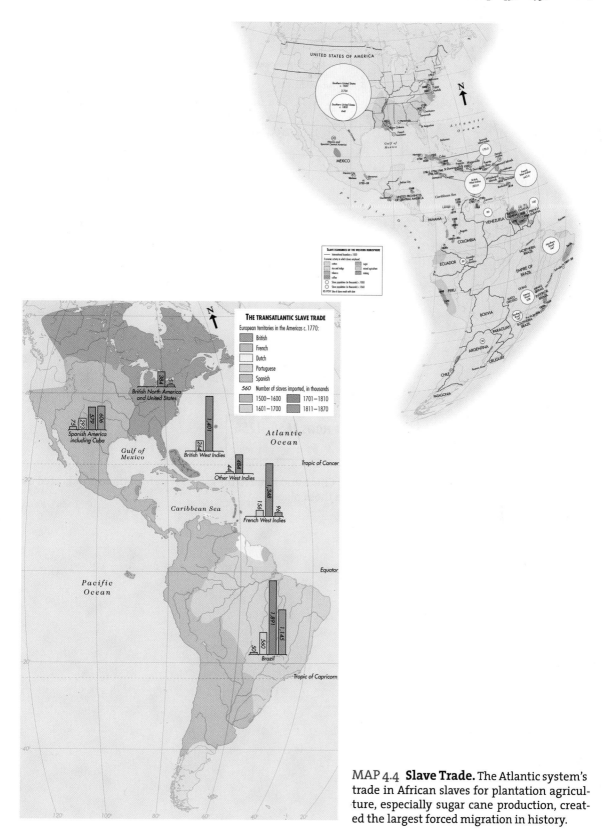

MAP 4.4 **Slave Trade.** The Atlantic system's trade in African slaves for plantation agriculture, especially sugar cane production, created the largest forced migration in history.

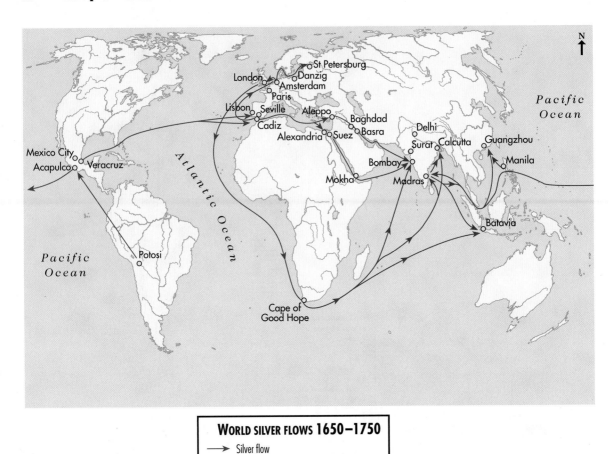

WORLD SILVER FLOWS 1650–1750
→ Silver flow

MAP 4.5 **World Silver Flows.** The centrality of China and India to the global system of trade is indicated by how much of the world's silver flows ended up in those places.

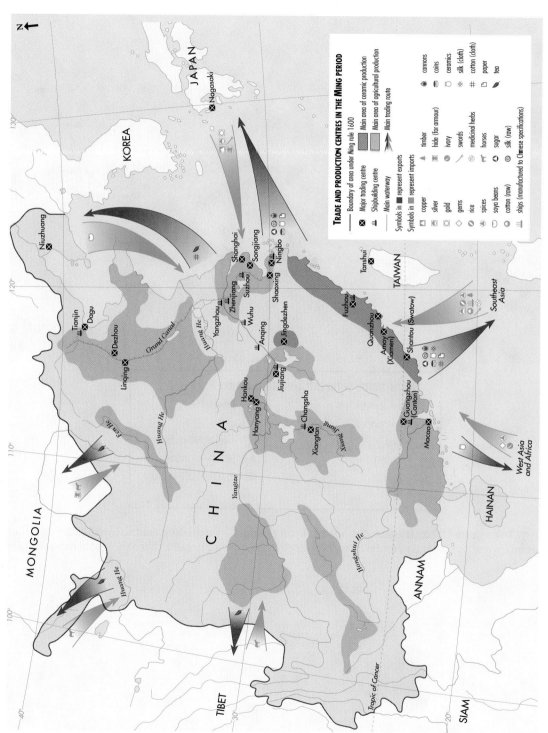

TRADE AND PRODUCTION CENTRES IN THE MING PERIOD

— Boundary of area under Ming rule 1600
■ Main area of ceramic production
■ Main area of agricultural production
↑ Main trading route

✖ Major trading centre
ℵ Shipbuilding centre
≈ Main waterway

Symbols in ■ represent exports
Symbols in ■ represent imports

copper	cannons		
silver	coins		
gold	timber	ceramics	
gems	hide (for armour)	silk (cloth)	
rice	ivory	cotton (cloth)	
spices	swords	paper	
soya beans	medicinal herbs	tea	
cotton (raw)	horses		
	sugar		
	silk (raw)		

ships (manufactured to Chinese specifications)

MONGOLIA

JAPAN

Nagasaki

KOREA

Niuzhuang

Tianjin
Dogu
Dezhou
Linqing

Grand Canal

Huang He
Fen He
Huang He

Huang He

TIBET

Tropic of Cancer

C H I N A

Yangtze

Hongshui He

Xiang Jiang

Han Jiang

Shanghai
Songjiang
Zhenjiang
Suzhou
Yangzhou
Wuhu
Anqing
Jingdezhen
Jiujiang
Hankou
Hanyang
Changsha
Xiangtan

Shaoxing
Ningbo

Fuzhou

Quanzhou
Amoy (Xiamen)
Shantou (Swatow)

Tanshui

TAIWAN

Southeast Asia

Guangzhou (Canton)
Macao

HAINAN

ANNAM

SIAM

West Asia and Africa

MAP 4.6 **Ming Trade and Production Centers.** The dynamic and varied Chinese economy was strongly connected to the global network despite official Chinese restrictions on the overseas activities of its own merchants.

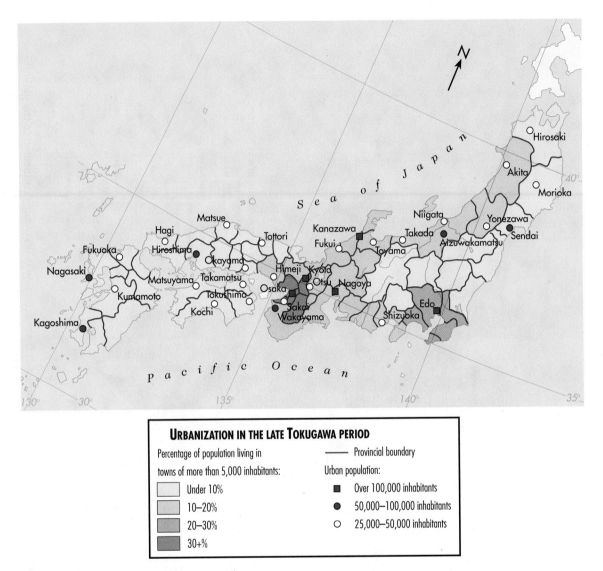

URBANIZATION IN THE LATE TOKUGAWA PERIOD

Percentage of population living in
towns of more than 5,000 inhabitants:

——— Provincial boundary

Urban population:

Under 10%	■ Over 100,000 inhabitants
10–20%	● 50,000–100,000 inhabitants
20–30%	○ 25,000–50,000 inhabitants
30+%	

MAP 4.7 **Tokugawa Urbanization.** Tokugawa Japan provides a fascinating contrast with China. Its internal economy grew significantly despite almost complete, self-imposed isolation from the global network after 1640.

States, Rulers, and Cultures

Against the background of global economic flows, traditional forms of imperial political organization continued to thrive. But the transformative impact of network flows began to affect cultures in various places and to lay the basis for significant political transformations.

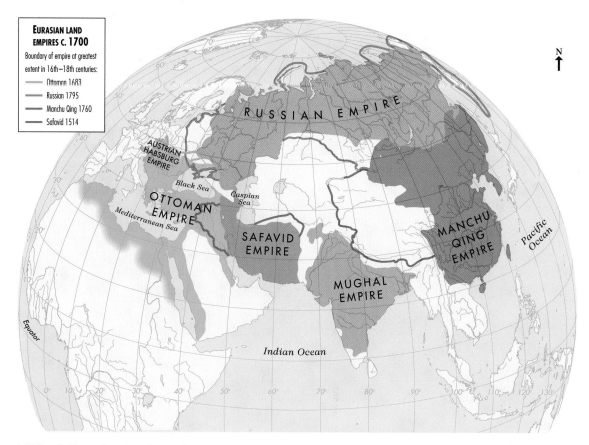

MAP 4.8 **Eurasian Land Empires, ca.1700.** The 17th and 18th centuries in Eurasia can be seen as a second "Age of Empires". Note that the success of these empires finally closed off and neutralized the nomadic pastoralists of central Asia as a major force.

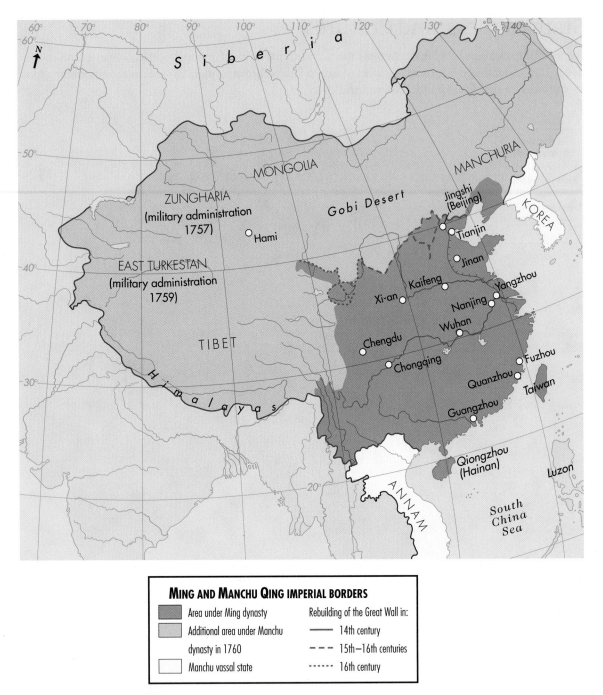

MING AND MANCHU QING IMPERIAL BORDERS

⬛ Area under Ming dynasty	Rebuilding of the Great Wall in:
⬛ Additional area under Manchu	——— 14th century
dynasty in 1760	– – – 15th–16th centuries
☐ Manchu vassal state	······· 16th century

MAP 4.9 **Ming and Manchu.** The closing of the steppes was the work of states that actually synthesized nomadic and sedentary military strengths. The semi-nomadic Manchus, who overthrew the Ming Dynasty in 1644, built such a system that allowed them to dominate vast areas of central Asia.

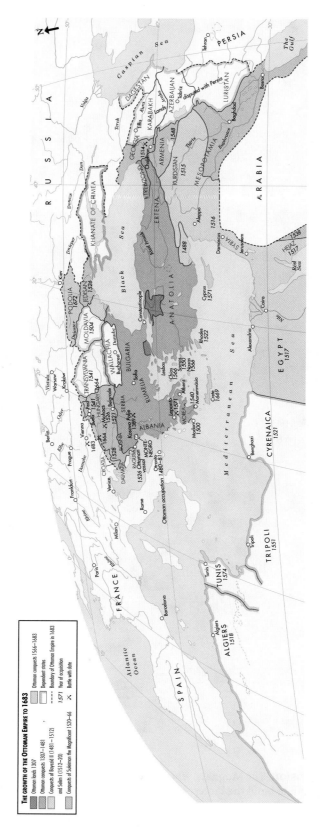

MAP 4.10 **Growth of the Ottoman Empire.** The Ottoman Turks, whose origins were nomadic but who ruled a rich sedentary empire, also used the complementary strengths of nomadic cavalry and sedentary infantry armed with muskets and cannon to build a successful empire.

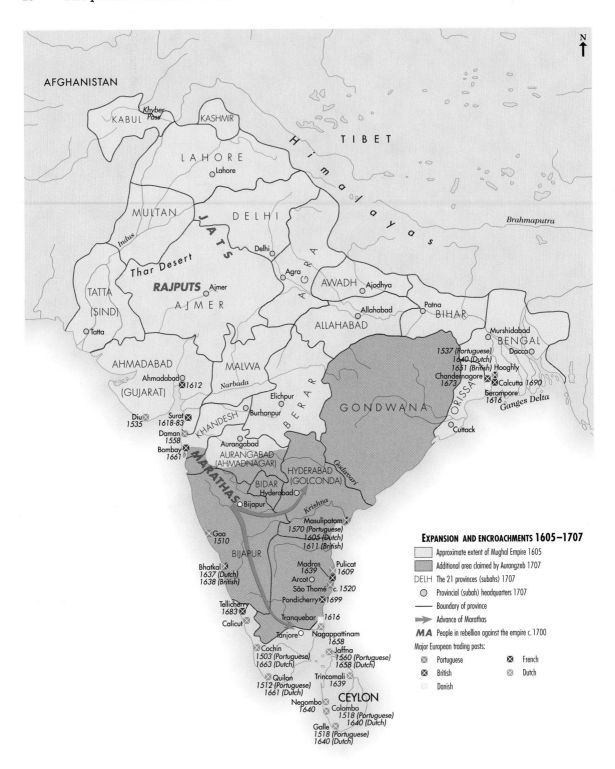

MAP 4.11 **Mughal Expansion.** The Mughals, whose origins lay on the steppes like the Ottomans', used the same sort of military system to build the largest sub-continental empire since the Mauryas.

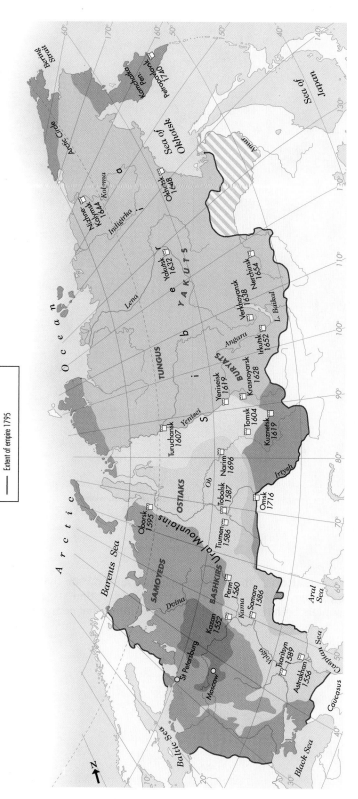

MAP 4.12 **Russian Expansion.** The Russian Empire, too, expanded by combining Cossack steppe cavalry with drilled infantry. But Russian merchants and settlers also moved into the fur-trading regions of Siberia, subjugating native hunter-gatherers and in effect colonizing the network itself.

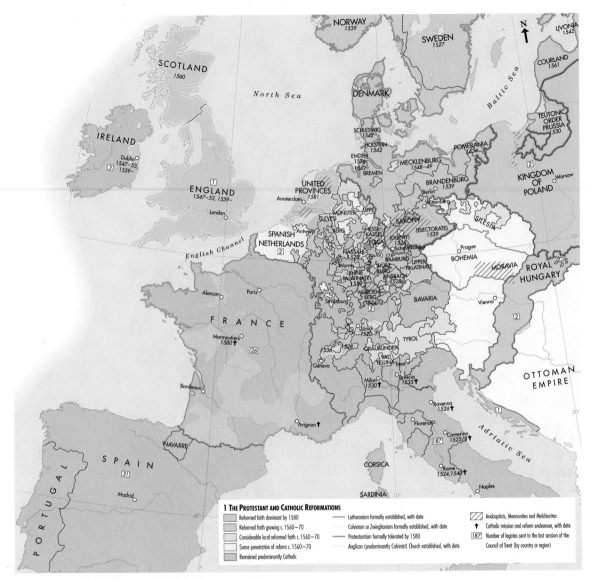

MAP 4.13 **Reformations.** The religious upheaval and warfare that accompanied the Protestant Reformation and the Catholic responses to it, the Catholic Reformation and the Counter-Reformation, illustrate the cultural encounters, both intra-cultural and inter-cultural, that occurred in a more globally networked world.

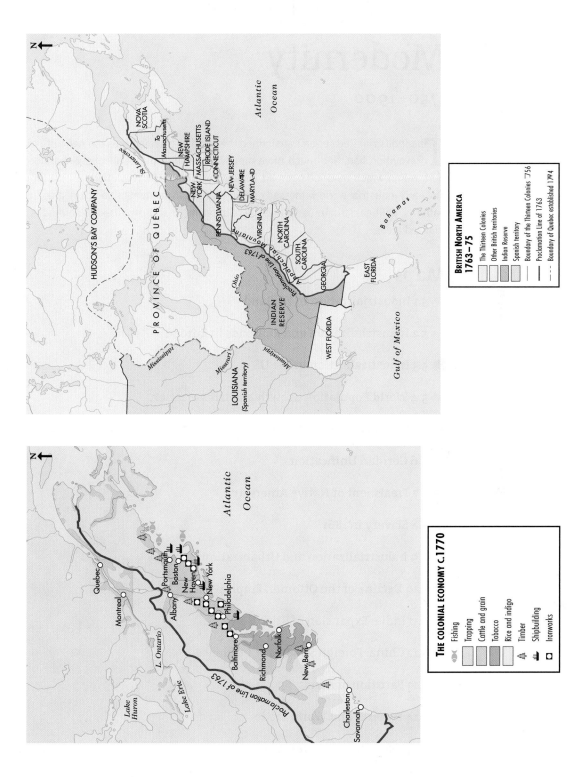

MAP 4.14 **American Colonies**. It was in British North America that globally-connected economic development and the peculiar structures of English political organization combined by 1776 to produce revolutionary political results. Even more fundamental revolutions would soon follow.

PART FIVE

The Origins of Modernity

1750–1900

The Industrial Revolution transformed the world as thoroughly as the Agricultural Revoultion had, and much more rapidly because of the developed global network within which (and in large part because of which) the revolution had started. The early industrial world witnessed drastic changes in economics and demographic patterns, political structures, and in the relationship of industrialized to non-industrialized areas.

Maps

▶ 5.1 Industrialization in England

▶ 5.2 Industrialization and Railroads in Europe

▶ 5.3 Industrialization in the US

▶ 5.4 World Population Growth and Urbanization

▶ 5.5 Major Population Movements, 1500-1914

▶ 5.6 German Unification

▶ 5.7 Treatment of Native Americans

▶ 5.8 Slavery in 1861

▶ 5.9 Industrialization and Urbanization in Japan

▶ 5.10 Decline of the Ottoman Empire

▶ 5.11 India: Expansion of British Empire

▶ 5.12 China: Foreign Spheres of Influence

▶ 5.13 Partition of Africa

▶ 5.14 Empires and World Trade

▶ 5.15 International Investment, 1914

Economic Revolution

Steam-powered industry spread from England to a limited set of other countries in the 19th century, but none-theless began to transform the entire world. Industrial jobs and transport initiated, for example, vast changes in living patterns and the balance of urban and rural life worldwide.

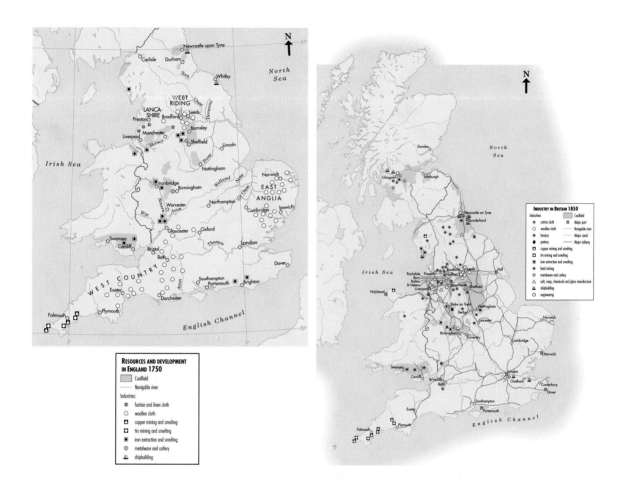

MAP 5.1 **Industrialization in England.** Between 1750 and 1850 Britain developed as the world's first industrial power.

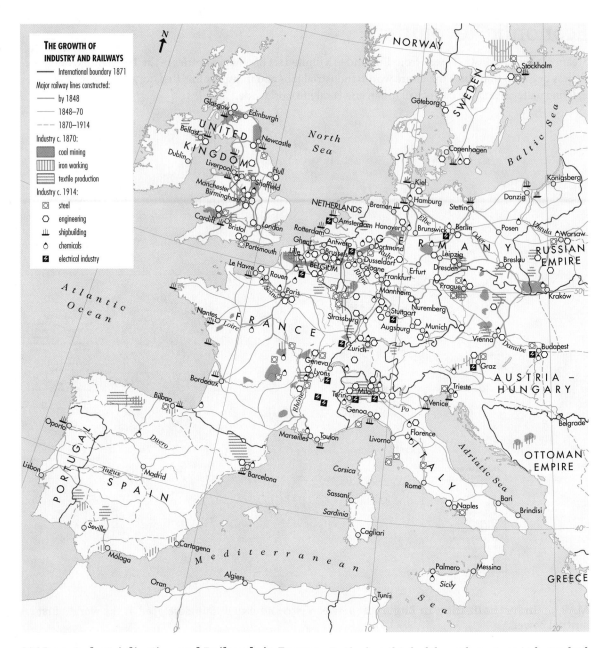

MAP 5.2 **Industrialization and Railroads in Europe.** By the last third of the 19th century, industry had spread to significant parts of continental Europe.

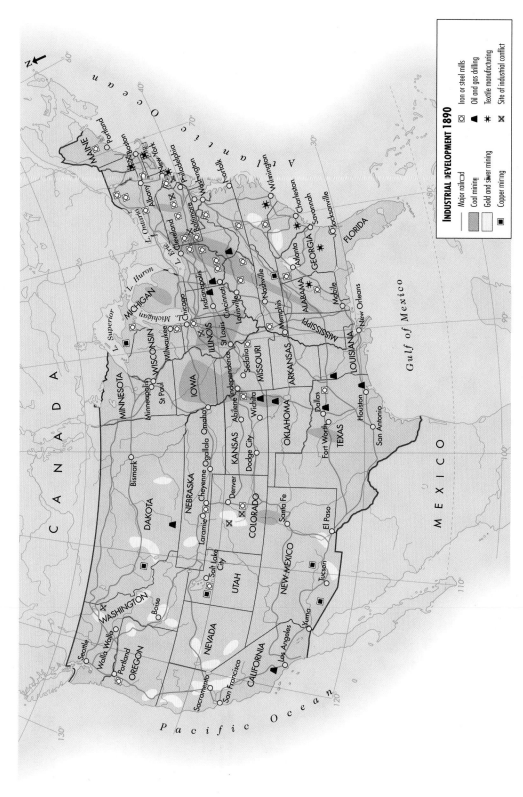

INDUSTRIAL DEVELOPMENT 1890

—— Major railroad	⊙ Iron or steel mills
Coal mining	▲ Oil and gas drilling
Gold and silver mining	✳ Textile manufacturing
■ Copper mining	✖ Site of industrial conflict

MAP 5.3 **Industrialization in the US.** The US, building on a heritage of British political and legal structures and aided by British investment, also industrialized heavily after 1865.

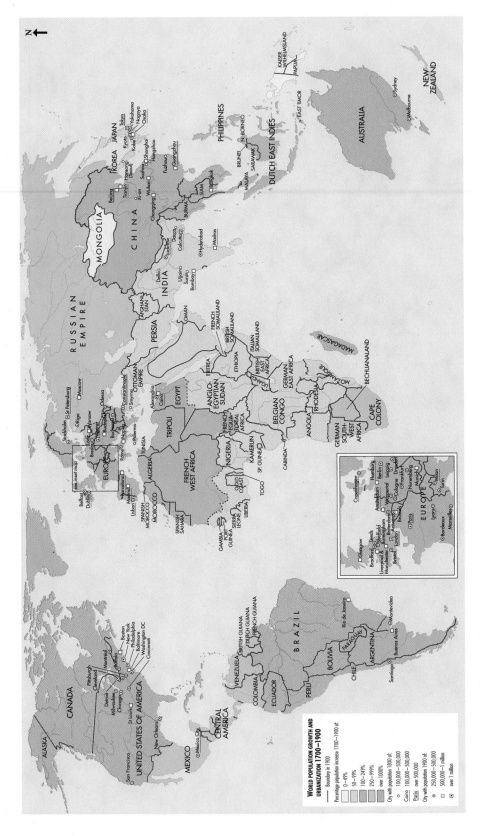

MAP 5.4 **World Population Growth and Urbanization.** Industry facilitated vast population growth. By 1900, 1 in 3 of the world's population was of European origin. That figure had been 1 in 5 in 1800, and would return to 1 in 5 by 2000.

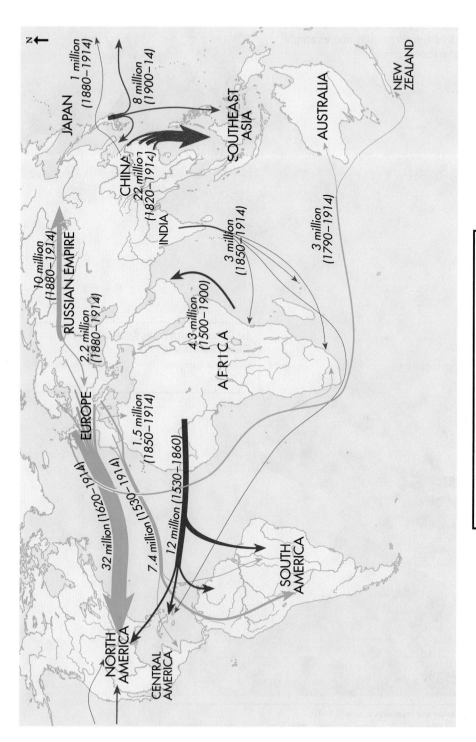

N

JAPAN   1 million
(1880–1914)

8 million
(1900–14)

SOUTHEAST
ASIA

CHINA
22 million
(1820–1914)

INDIA

AUSTRALIA

NEW
ZEALAND

3 million
(1850–1914)

3 million
(1790–1914)

10 million
(1880–1914)

RUSSIAN EMPIRE

2.2 million
(1880–1914)

EUROPE

4.3 million
(1500–1900)

AFRICA

1.5 million
(1850–1914)

32 million (1620–1914)

7.4 million (1530–1914)

12 million (1530–1860)

NORTH
AMERICA

CENTRAL
AMERICA

SOUTH
AMERICA

MAJOR POPULATION MOVEMENTS 1500–1914

Migration originating from:

—— Asia

—— Europe, Scandinavia and western Russia

—— Africa

MAP 5.5 **Major Population Movements, 1500-1914.** Population growth was accompanied by massive migrations of population, especially out of Europe.

MAP 5.6 **German Unification.** Nationalism proved perhaps the most potent new ideology of the industrial age. While it threatened multi-national empires such as Austria-Hungary, political leaders in Prussia deployed nationalism to help create a united Germany, just one example from many of the power of nationalism.

THE GERMAN CONFEDERATION, AUSTRIAN EMPIRE, PRUSSIA AND DENMARK 1815		
Austrian Habsburg Empire		Border of German Confederation
Prussia		Denmark

GERMANY FROM CONFEDERATION TO EMPIRE 1815–71				
Habsburg Empire	Border of German Customs Union (Zollverein) 1842	A	Anhalt	MS Mecklenburg-Strelitz
Prussia 1815	Southern border of North German Confederation 1867	B	Brunswick	O Oldenburg
Territory added to Prussia 1815–66	Border of German Empire 1871	Ha	Hamburg	P Prussia
Territory added to Prussia/ German Empire 1871		H	Hanover	TS Thuringian States

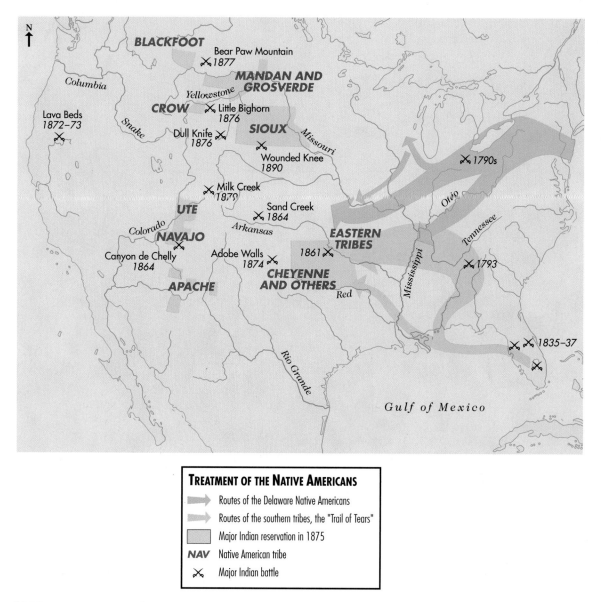

TREATMENT OF THE NATIVE AMERICANS

➡ Routes of the Delaware Native Americans

➡ Routes of the southern tribes, the "Trail of Tears"

▢ Major Indian reservation in 1875

NAV Native American tribe

✕ Major Indian battle

MAP 5.7 **Treatment of Native Americans.** The demographic and economic expansion of the US occurred at the expense of the Native American population.

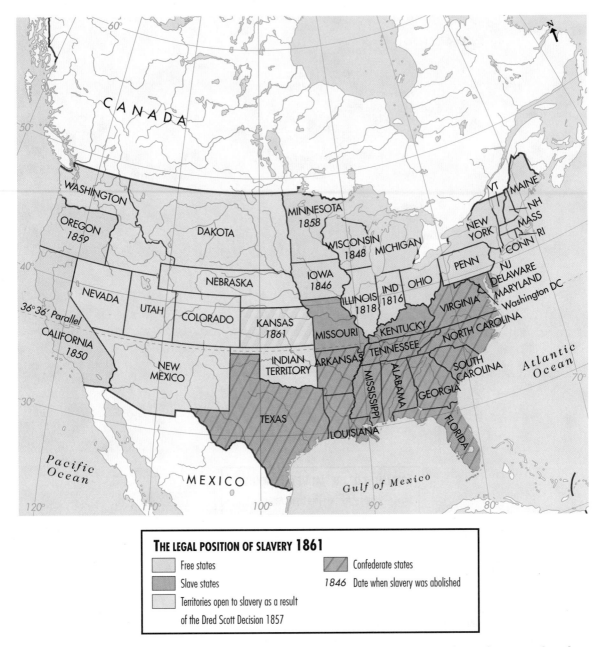

THE LEGAL POSITION OF SLAVERY 1861

- Free states
- Slave states
- Territories open to slavery as a result of the Dred Scott Decision 1857
- Confederate states
- *1846* Date when slavery was abolished

MAP 5.8 **Slavery in the United States in 1861.** Slavery divided the US into an industrializing north and an agrarian south, creating intractable political conflict that led to the Civil War.

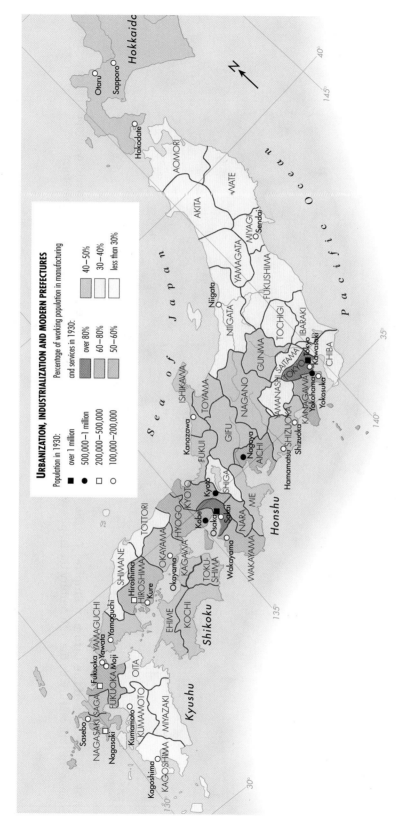

URBANIZATION, INDUSTRIALIZATION AND MODERN PREFECTURES

Population in 1930:

■ over 1 million

■ 500,000–1 million

□ 200,000–500,000

○ 100,000–200,000

Percentage of working population in manufacturing and services in 1930:

over 80%

60–80%

50–60%

40–50%

30–40%

less than 30%

MAP 5.9 **Japan: Industrialization and Urbanization.** Japan met the threat of western industrial imperialism by revolutionizing its own political structures and successfully industrializing.

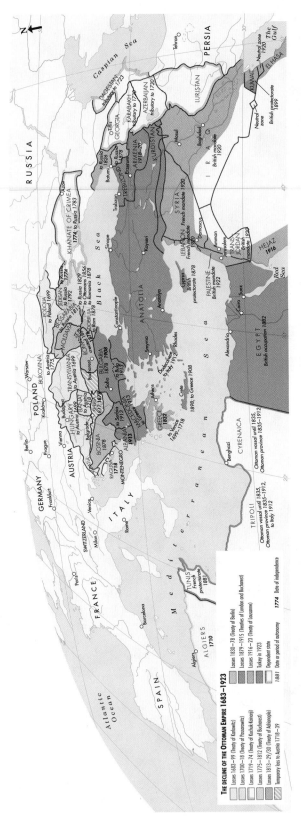

MAP 5.10 **Decline of the Ottoman Empire.** The Ottoman Empire faced challenges in keeping pace with the western European pace of change even in the 18th century. By the 19th century the Empire was in serious decline despite several attempts at internal reform

Industrial Imperialism

The vastly increasing the economic and military power of industrializing countries, combined with national-ist-inspired competition, led to an explosion of imperialism in the last third of the 19ᵗʰ century, one aspect of the first great wave of industrially-driven globalization.

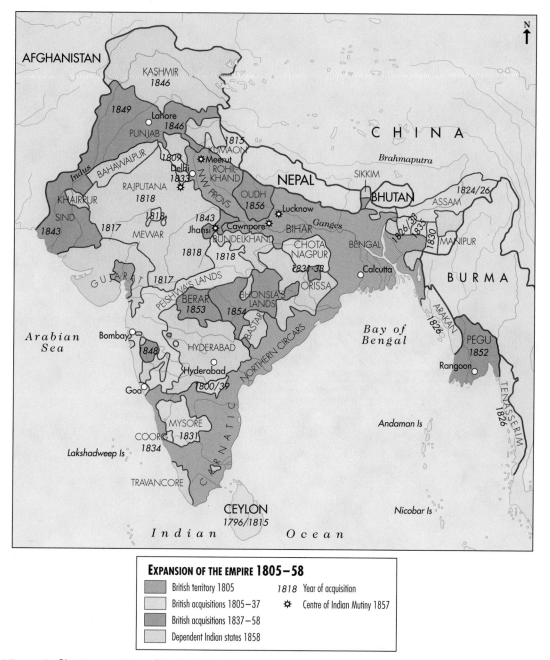

EXPANSION OF THE EMPIRE 1805–58		
▇ British territory 1805	*1818*	Year of acquisition
▢ British acquisitions 1805–37	✻	Centre of Indian Mutiny 1857
▇ British acquisitions 1837–58		
▢ Dependent Indian states 1858		

MAP 5.11 **India: Expansion of British Empire.** The British Empire in India predated industrialization, but the growth of British industry transformed the economic relationship of colonizer and colonized and encouraged expansion of British rule.

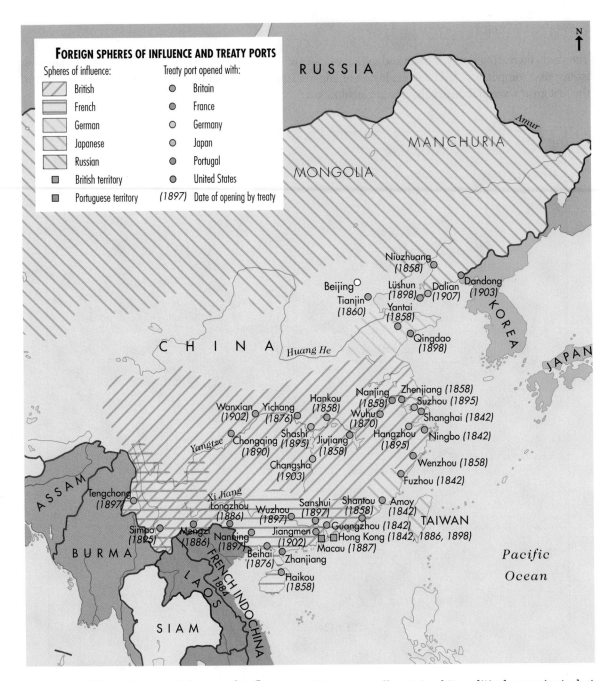

FOREIGN SPHERES OF INFLUENCE AND TREATY PORTS

Spheres of influence:

- British
- French
- German
- Japanese
- Russian
- British territory
- Portuguese territory

Treaty port opened with:

- Britain
- France
- Germany
- Japan
- Portugal
- United States

(1897) Date of opening by treaty

RUSSIA

MONGOLIA

MANCHURIA

Amur

CHINA

Huang He

KOREA

JAPAN

Beijing
Tianjin *(1860)*
Niuzhuang *(1858)*
Lüshun *(1898)*
Yantai *(1858)*
Dalian *(1907)*
Dandong *(1903)*
Qingdao *(1898)*

Nanjing *(1858)*
Zhenjiang *(1858)*
Suzhou *(1895)*
Hankou *(1858)*
Wuhu *(1870)*
Shanghai *(1842)*
Wanxian *(1902)* Yichang *(1876)*
Shashi *(1895)*
Hangzhou *(1895)*
Ningbo *(1842)*
Chongqing *(1890)* Jiujiang *(1858)*
Changsha *(1903)*
Wenzhou *(1858)*
Fuzhou *(1842)*

Yangtze

ASSAM

Tengchong *(1897)*

Xi Jiang
Longzhou *(1886)*
Wuzhou *(1897)*
Sanshui *(1897)*
Shantou *(1858)*
Amoy *(1842)*
TAIWAN

Simao *(1895)*
Mengzi *(1886)*
Nanning *(1897)*
Jiangmen *(1902)*
Guangzhou *(1842)*
Hong Kong *(1842, 1886, 1898)*
Macau *(1887)*

BURMA

Beihai *(1876)*
Zhanjiang

LAOS
1884
FRENCH INDOCHINA

Haikou *(1858)*

SIAM

Pacific Ocean

MAP 5.12 **China: Foreign Spheres of Influence.** China nominally retained its political sovereignty, but the former heart of the global economy saw itself divided into spheres of economic influence within which foreign powers had extensive privileges.

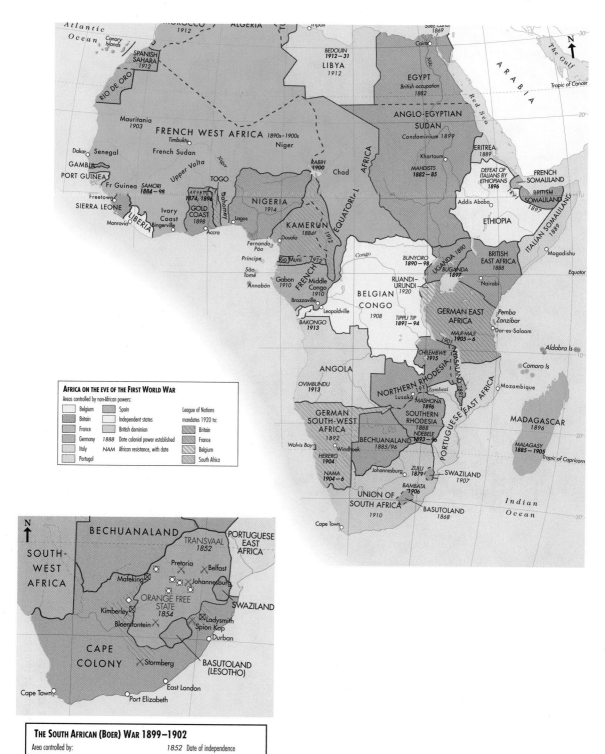

AFRICA ON THE EVE OF THE FIRST WORLD WAR

Areas controlled by non-African powers:

		League of Nations
Belgium	Spain	mandates 1920 to:
Britain	Independent states	Britain
France	British dominion	France
Germany 1888 Date colonial power established		Belgium
Italy NAM African resistance, with date		South Africa
Portugal		

THE SOUTH AFRICAN (BOER) WAR 1899–1902

Area controlled by:

	1852 Date of independence
Britain at outbreak of war	⊠ Siege by Afrikaners 1899–1900
Afrikaners (Boers) at outbreak of war	✕ Afrikaner victory 1899–1900
Afrikaners 1899–1900	✕ British victory 1900
Portugal	◇ Diamond mining
Germany	◉ Gold mining

MAP 5.13 **Partition of Africa.** The height of imperialist competition occurred in the "Scramble for Africa" between 1885 and 1914.

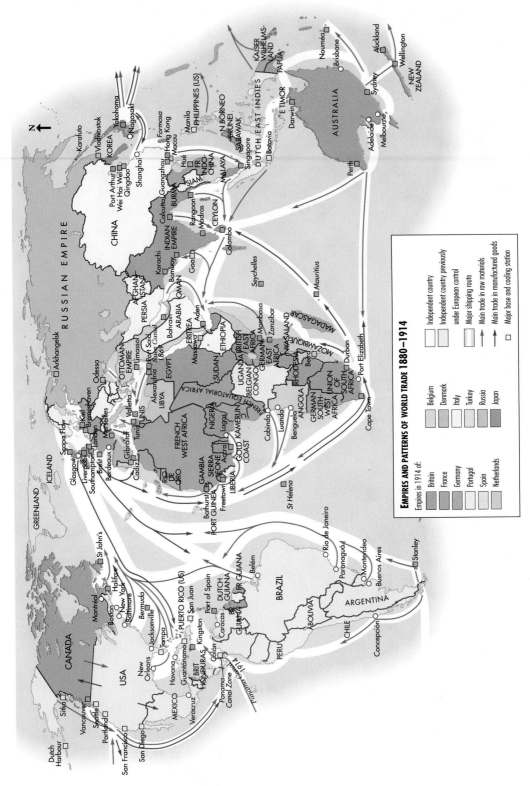

MAP 5.14 Empires and World Trade. The economic motivations for imperialism—need for raw materials and desire for new markets—are clearly reflected in the patterns of world trade in the age of imperialism.

EMPIRES AND PATTERNS OF WORLD TRADE 1880–1914

Empires in 1914 of:

Britain	Belgium
France	Denmark
Germany	Italy
Portugal	Turkey
Spain	Russia
Netherlands	Japan

- Independent country
- Independent country previously under European control
- Major shipping route
- Main trade in raw materials
- Main trade in manufactured goods
- Major base and cooling station

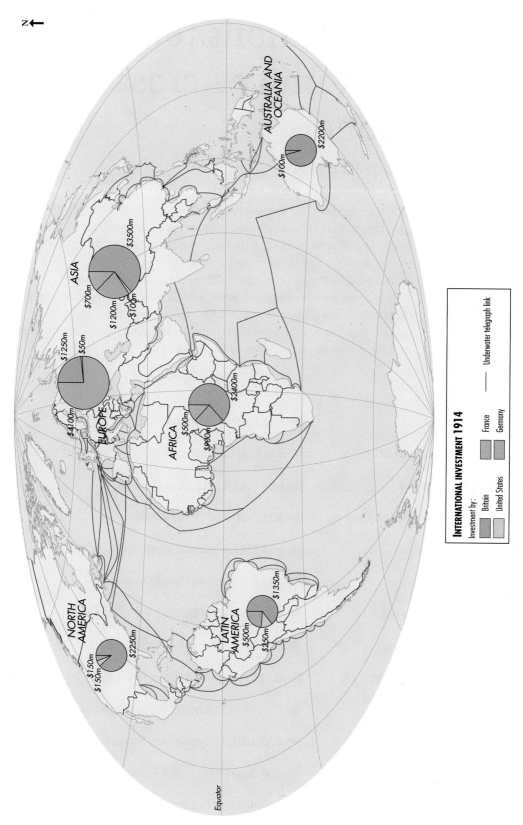

MAP 5.15 **International Investment, 1914.** Patterns of international investment—dominated by British capital in most regions—can be traced along the expanding network of undersea telegraph links.

PART SIX Adaptations to Modernity Across the Globe

1900–PRESENT

The social, political, and economic tensions created by 19th century industrialization (and its uneven spread across the world) exploded in the industrial heartland of Europe in 1914, initiating nearly a century of conflict over the shape and values of the new industrial world system.

The many military and political conflicts of the 20th century tend to obscure an underlying history of demographic and economic growth that began to have increasing effects on the global environment. Economic development also created its own new political patterns, and since 1970 the second great wave of industrial globalization has transformed societies and cultures around the world.

Maps

World War I and Political Upheaval

Essentially a civil war among the great European industrial powers, World War I was a world war by virtue of those powers' global influence. It brought the transitional political structures of the early industrial 19th century, mostly still monarchical in one form or another, crashing down, and initiated a round of political and ideological revolutions.

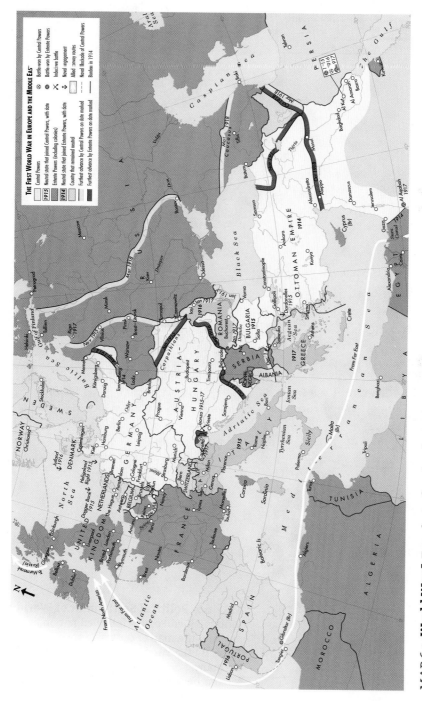

MAP 6.1 **World War I.** Trench warfare dominates images of World War I, and the Western Front in France was indeed largely a bloody stalemate. But other theaters, especially in Russia, saw more movement.

TREATY SETTLEMENTS IN EUROPE 1919–23

Boundary 1923
Pre-war boundary
Territory administered by League of Nations
Demilitarized zone
1918 Date of independence

TREATIES BETWEEN ENTENTE POWERS AND DEFEATED COUNTRIES:
Treaty of Versailles 28 June 1919 — Entente Powers (excluding USA) and Germany
Treaty of Saint-Germain 10 September 1919 — Entente Powers and Austria
Treaty of Neuilly 24 November 1919 — Entente Powers and Bulgaria
Treaty of Trianon 4 June 1920 — Entente Powers and Hungary
Treaty of Sèvres 10 August 1920 — Entente Powers (excluding USA and USSR) and Turkey (Sultanate of), superseded by:
Treaty of Lausanne 24 July 1923 with Turkish Republic
Treaty of Berlin 2 July 1921 — USA and Germany

EUROPE IN 1914

Russian Empire
Austro-Hungarian Empire

MAP 6.2 **Political Settlement of World War I.** The victorious Allied Powers followed nationalist principles in redrawing the map of central Europe in the wake of the war. This, and the harsh economic retribution they imposed on Germany, poisoned the peace and created conditions ripe for another round of fighting.

MAP 6.3 **Soviet Union, 1928-39.** Revolution and civil war in Russia from 1917 gave birth to the Soviet Union, the world's first avowedly communist power. The USSR's economic success in the 1930s, while the capitalist powers suffered through the Great Depression, disguised the tyranny of Stalin's rule.

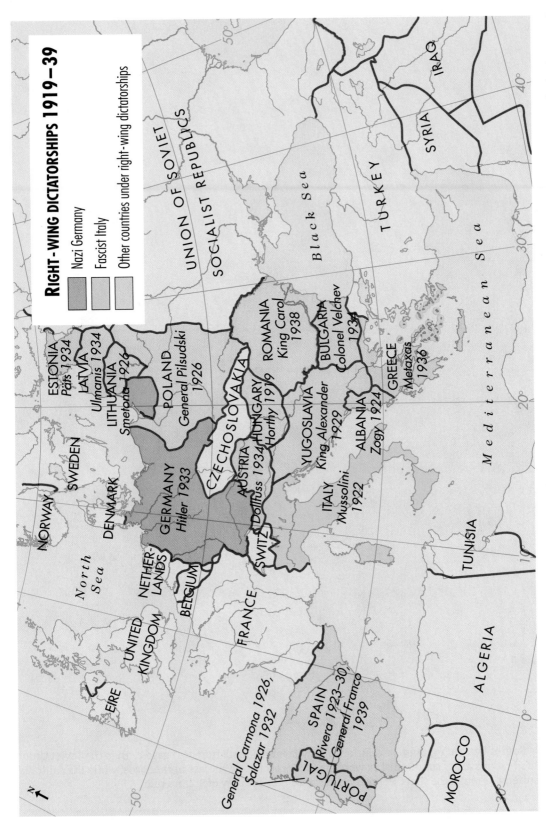

MAP 6.4 **Right Wing Dictatorships, 1919–39.** Partly in reaction to the emergence of the USSR, fascism and related right-wing ideologies swept across the political map of Europe in the 1930's.

The Great Depression and World War II

The post-World War I world collapsed into economic depression in 1929, further destabilizing political relationships. When the Japanese, who had already taken over Manchuria, invaded China in 1947, the world descended into a truly global conflict.

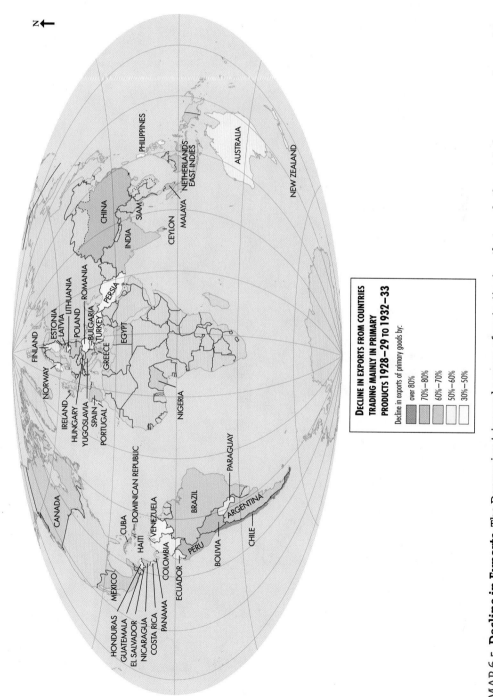

MAP 6.5 **Decline in Exports.** The Depression triggered a wave of protectionism that made the crisis far worse and spread its effects far beyond the industrial countries. World trade collapsed, impoverishing societies dependent on exporting raw materials.

DECLINE IN EXPORTS FROM COUNTRIES TRADING MAINLY IN PRIMARY PRODUCTS 1928–29 TO 1932–33

Decline in exports of primary goods by:

- over 80%
- 70%–80%
- 60%–70%
- 50%–60%
- 30%–50%

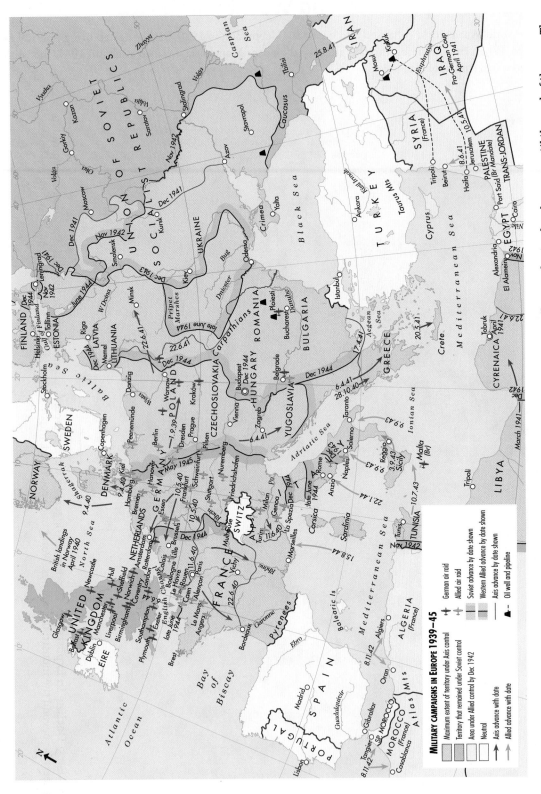

MAP 6.6 **World War II in Europe.** Axis conquests came to a halt by 1942, and the Allies made steady advances until the end of the war. The USSR (20 million dead) bore the brunt of the European fight against Nazi Germany.

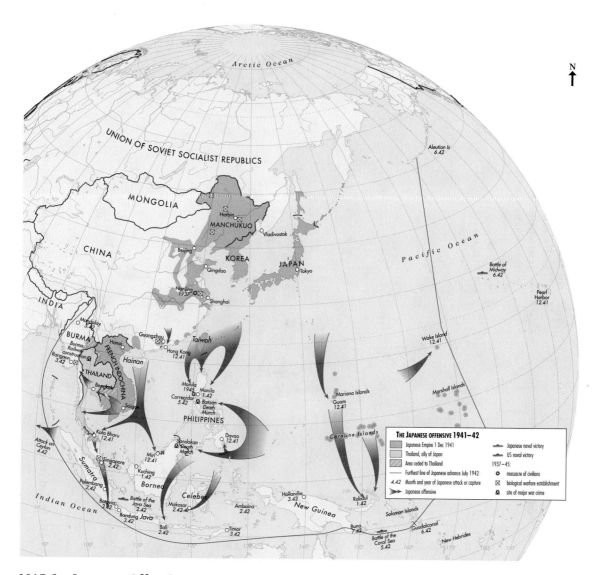

N
↑

MAP 6.7 **Japanese Offensive, 1941-1942.** Japanese expansion aimed at securing resources unavailable in Japan itself and creating a defensive cordon around the empire.

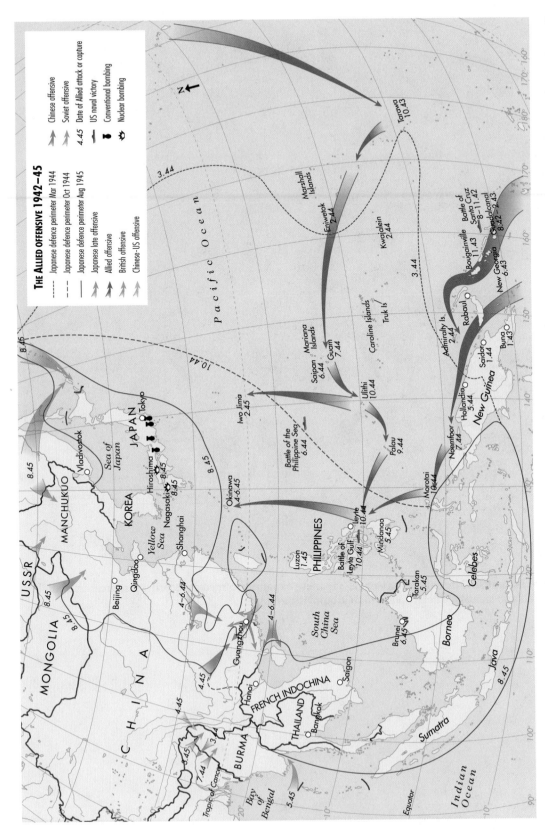

MAP 6.8 **Allied Pacific Offensive, 1942-1945.** The US-led counter-offensive benefitted from the US's vast advantages in industrial capacity and access to resources.

The Cold War and Decolonization

The victorious Allies split almost immediately after the war into two camps, capitalist and communist, led by the US and the USSR, respectively. The two major powers never went to war directly with each other, competing economically, culturally, and politically in a long "Cold War". But both powers fought through and with proxies. Cold War dynamics complicated the process of deconstructing 19th century empires whose foundations had been fatally weakened by the two World Wars.

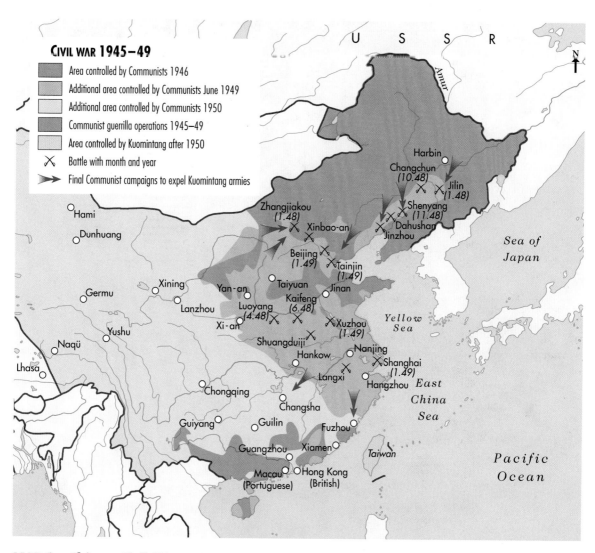

MAP 6.9 **Chinese Civil War, 1945-49.** The Communist world expanded dramatically when the Soviet-backed Chinese Communist Party defeated the US-backed Nationalists in a civil war that had been interrupted by World War II. But China soon came into conflict with the Soviet Union, complicating Cold War politics.

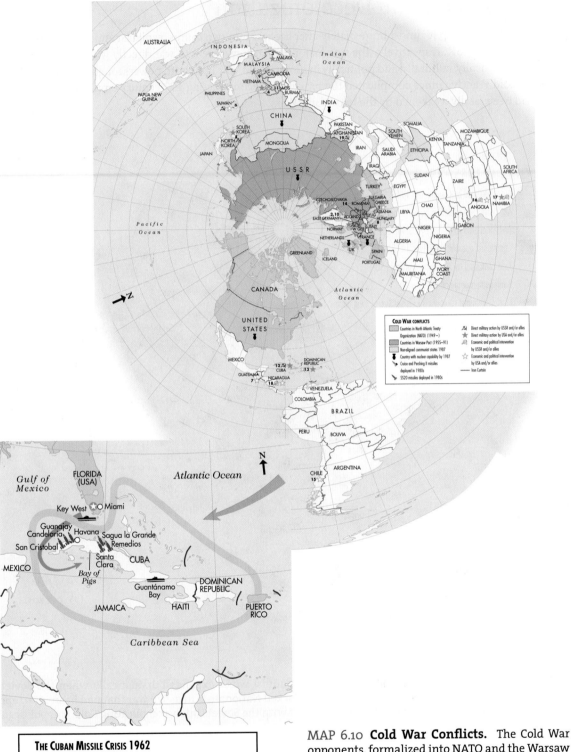

MAP 6.10 **Cold War Conflicts.** The Cold War opponents, formalized into NATO and the Warsaw Pact, faced each other not just in western Europe but, with the invention of intercontinental ballistic missiles, directly across the North Pole.

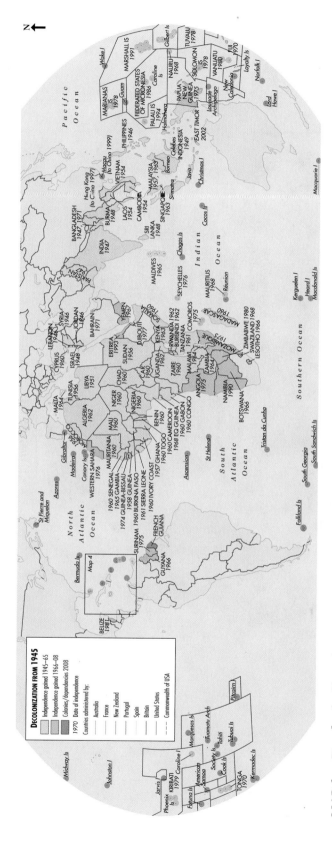

MAP 6.11 **Decolonization since 1945.** Complicated by the influence of Cold War dichotomies, decolonization nevertheless proceeded rapidly after 1945.

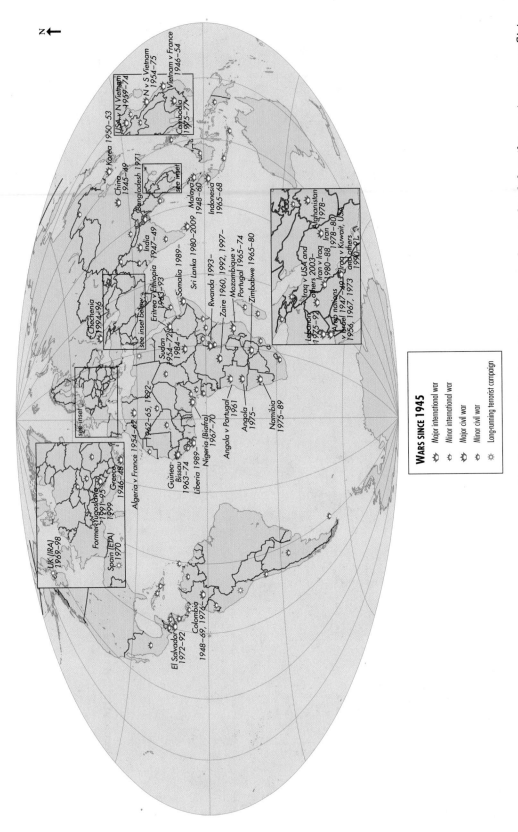

MAP 6.12 **Wars Since 1945.** Military conflict in the second half of the 20th century has been more decentralized than the great power conflicts before 1945. Small power conflicts, proxy wars, civil wars, and terrorist campaigns have dominated military operations.

Humans and the Environment

The human impact on the global environment had become so significant by the beginning of the 21st century that some scientists began identifying a new geological period, the "anthropocene"—the Age of Humans.

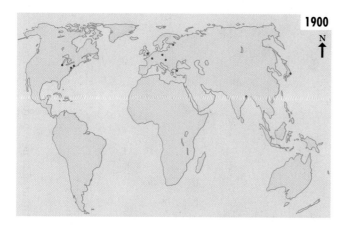

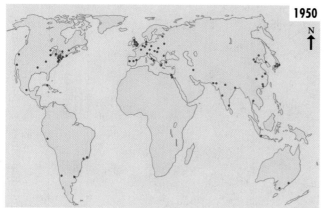

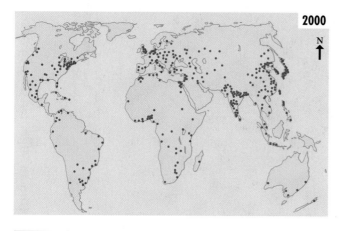

URBANIZATION OF THE WORLD
- City of at least 1 million inhabitants

MAP 6.13 **Urbanization of the World.** Massive population growth across the 20th century (seemingly undented by the mass destruction of life in warfare) was concentrated increasingly in cities. By 2010, more than half the world's population lived in cities.

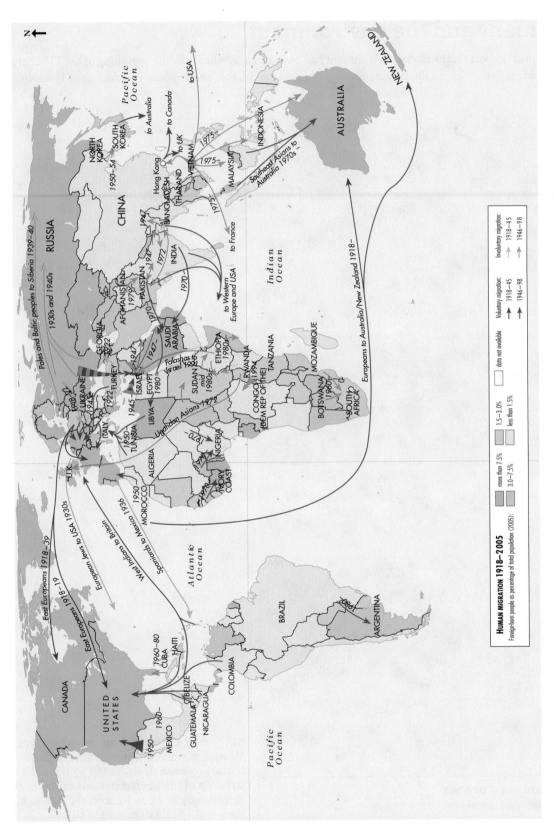

MAP 6.14 Human Migration since 1918. Economic disparities and political conflicts contributed to new patterns of human migration.

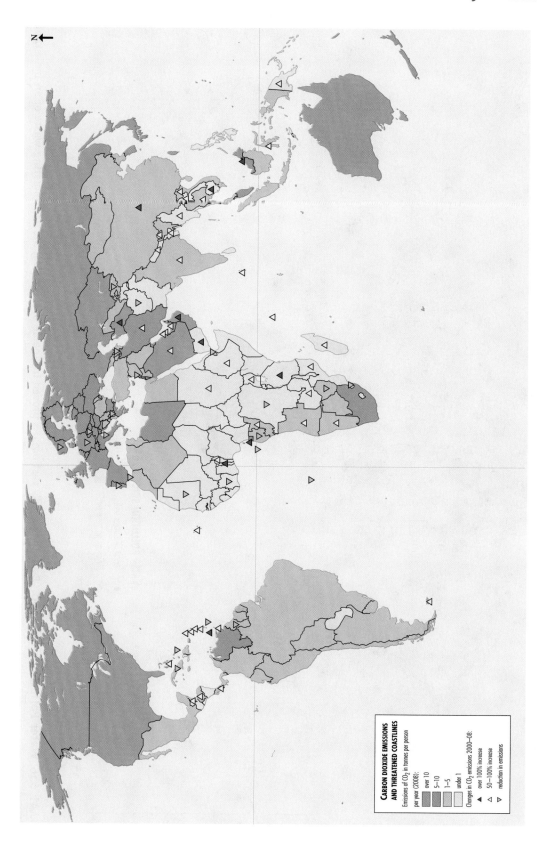

MAP 6.15 **CO² emissions.** Burning fossil fuels to power industry and its products (especially automobiles) releases carbon dioxide, a greenhouse gas, into the atmosphere, contributing to global warming.

CARBON DIOXIDE EMISSIONS AND THREATENED COASTLINES

Emissions of CO_2 in tonnes per person

per year (2008):

over 10

5–10

1–5

under 1

Changes in CO_2 emissions 2000–08:

▲ over 100% increase

◁ 50–100% increase

▽ reduction in emissions

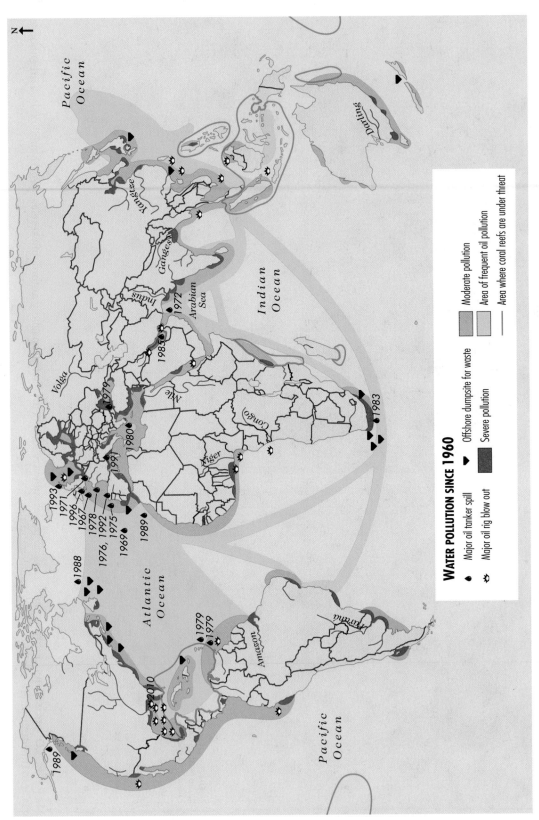

MAP 6.16 **Water Pollution since 1960.** Even the world's vast oceans proved incapable of absorbing the accumulating waste of an industrial world.

Economics and Politics

Economic growth has sometimes created political conflicts, but has also contributed to the spread of democracy globally.

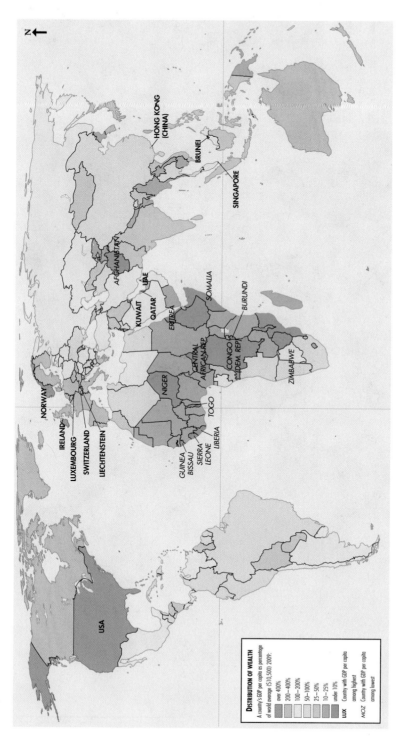

MAP 6.17 **Distribution of Wealth.** Distribution of wealth—not just between countries but within countries—has probably been the central political issue of the industrial era. Generally, inequalities create instability.

DISTRIBUTION OF WEALTH

A country's GDP per capita as percentage of world average ($10,500) 2009:

- over 400%
- 200–400%
- 100–200%
- 50–100%
- 25–50%
- 10–25%
- under 10%

LUX Country with GDP per capita among highest

MOZ Country with GDP per capita among lowest

MAP 6.18 **EU Economic Integration.** The European Union provides one model of economic union leading to political integration and the decline of war among member states, however recent financial crises have put a strain on the EU.

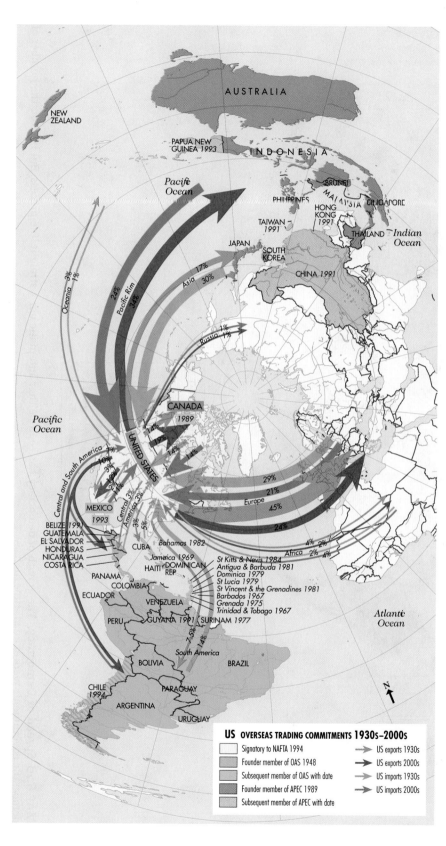

NEW
ZEALAND

AUSTRALIA

PAPUA NEW
GUINEA 1993

INDONESIA

*Pacific
Ocean*

BRUNEI

PHILIPPINES

MALAYSIA

SINGAPORE

TAIWAN
1991

HONG
KONG
1991

JAPAN

SOUTH
KOREA

THAILAND

*Indian
Ocean*

CHINA 1991

3% 3%
Oceania
1%

26%
Pacific Rim
34%

17%
Asia
30%

Russia
1%
1%

*Pacific
Ocean*

CANADA
1989

UNITED STATES

14%
9%
14%   14%

29%
21%
Europe
45%

24%

Central and South America
10%
3%
2%

Central 3%
America 3%

MEXICO
1993

Central 3%
America 3%
5%

Africa
4% 2%
2%   4%

BELIZE 1991
GUATEMALA
EL SALVADOR
HONDURAS
NICARAGUA
COSTA RICA

CUBA

Bahamas 1982

Jamaica 1969

DOMINICAN
REP

St Kitts & Nevis 1984
Antigua & Barbuda 1981
Dominica 1979
St Lucia 1979
St Vincent & the Grenadines 1981
Barbados 1967
Grenada 1975
Trinidad & Tobago 1967

PANAMA

HAITI

COLOMBIA

ECUADOR

VENEZUELA

PERU

GUYANA 1991

SURINAM 1977

*Atlantic
Ocean*

7.5%
14%

South America

BOLIVIA

BRAZIL

N

CHILE
1994

PARAGUAY

ARGENTINA

URUGUAY

US OVERSEAS TRADING COMMITMENTS **1930s–2000s**

- Signatory to NAFTA 1994
- Founder member of OAS 1948
- Subsequent member of OAS with date
- Founder member of APEC 1989
- Subsequent member of APEC with date

→ US exports 1930s
→ US exports 2000s
→ US imports 1930s
→ US imports 2000s

MAP 6.19 **US Overseas Trade, 1930's-2000's.** The US economy occupied a central position in the world economy for much of the 20th century.

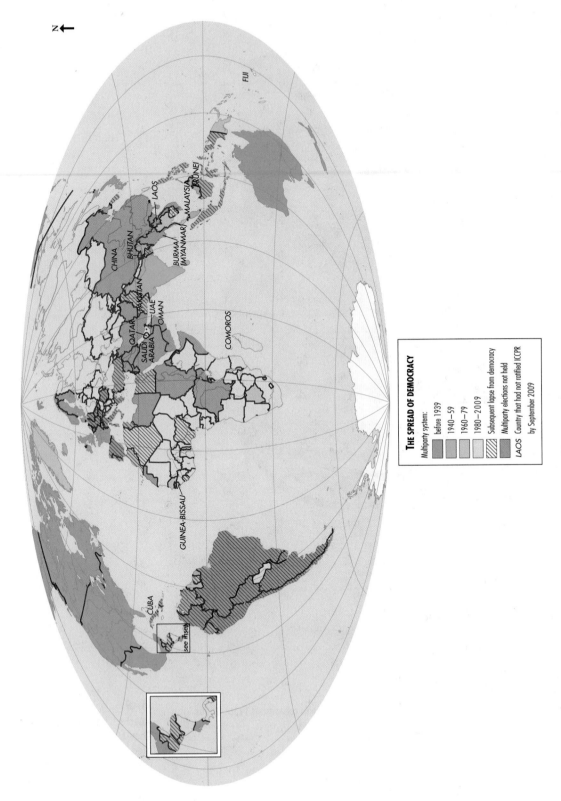

MAP 6.20 **Spread of Democracy.** The growth of democracy has been neither automatic nor a straight line process. But by 2010 the number of democratic governments were at an all-time high.

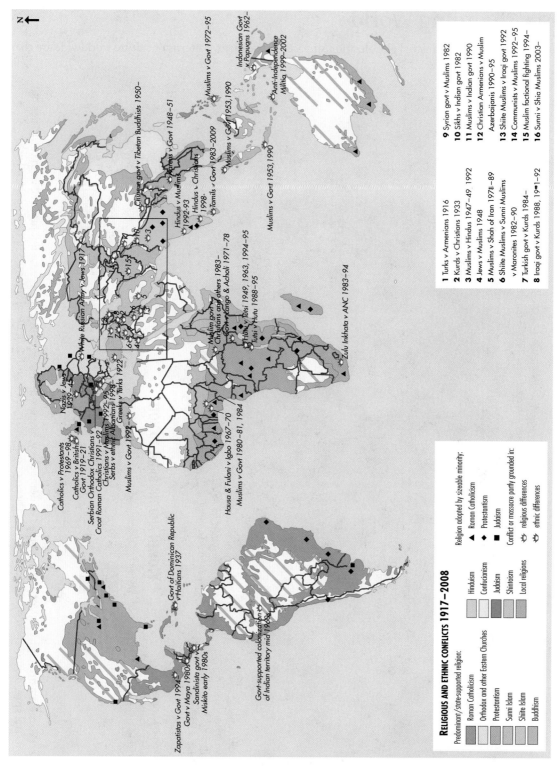

MAP 6.21 **Religious and Ethnic Conflicts, 1917-2008.** Economic integration and democracy face countervailing tendencies toward division fostered by religious and ethnic differences, the latter expressed in a resurgence of ethnic nationalism since 1989.

One Changing World

As the second wave of industrial globalization spreads and deepens, patterns of culture worldwide are changing.

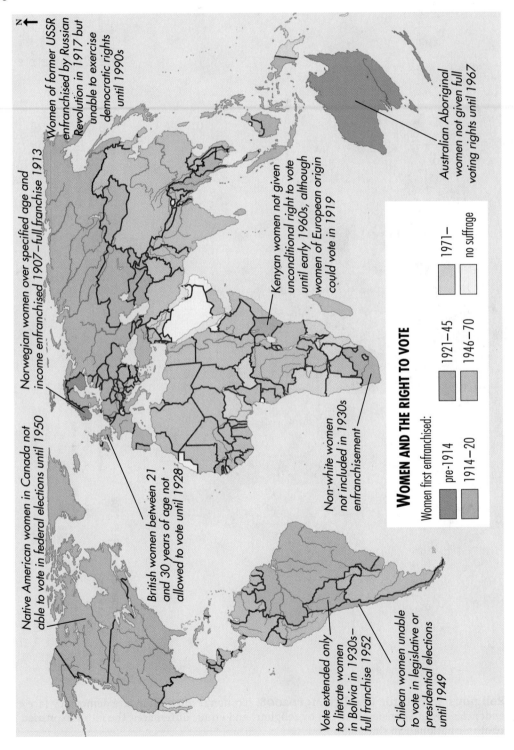

Women of former USSR enfranchised by Russian Revolution in 1917 but unable to exercise democratic rights until 1990s

Norwegian women over specified age and income enfranchised 1907—full franchise 1913

Australian Aboriginal women not given full voting rights until 1967

Kenyan women not given unconditional right to vote until early 1960s, although women of European origin could vote in 1919

Native American women in Canada not able to vote in federal elections until 1950

British women between 21 and 30 years of age not allowed to vote until 1928

Non-white women not included in 1930s enfranchisement

Vote extended only to literate women in Bolivia in 1930s—full franchise 1952

Chilean women unable to vote in legislative or presidential elections until 1949

WOMEN AND THE RIGHT TO VOTE

Women first enfranchised:

- pre-1914
- 1914—20
- 1921—45
- 1946—70
- 1971—
- no suffrage

MAP 6.22 **Women and Right to Vote.** The spread of democracy, like economic equality, is an issue not just between countries but inside them. The spread of women's political rights has been one of the most significant developments of the industrial era.

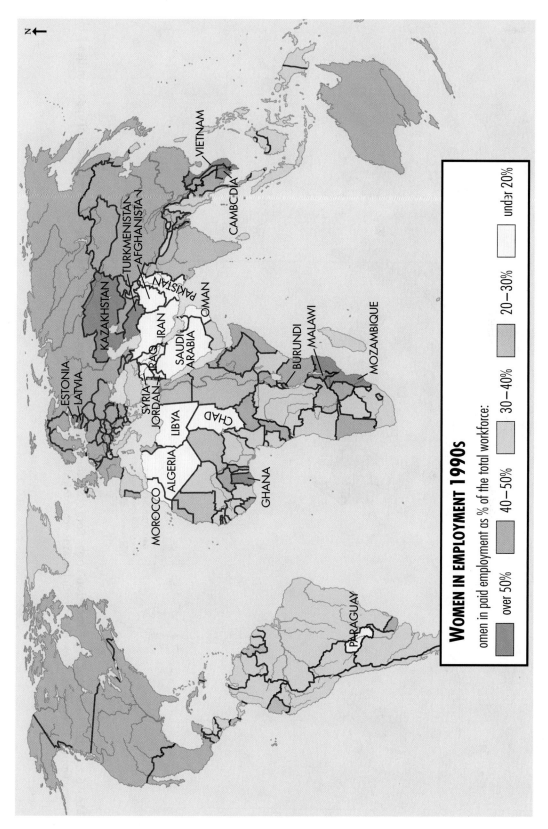

WOMEN IN EMPLOYMENT 1990s

omen in paid employment as % of the total workforce:

over 50%	30–40%	under 20%
40–50%	20–30%	

MAP 6.23 **Women in Employment 1990s.** The reciprocal relationship between economic rights and opportunities on the one hand and political rights on the other show up particularly clearly in patterns of female employment globally.

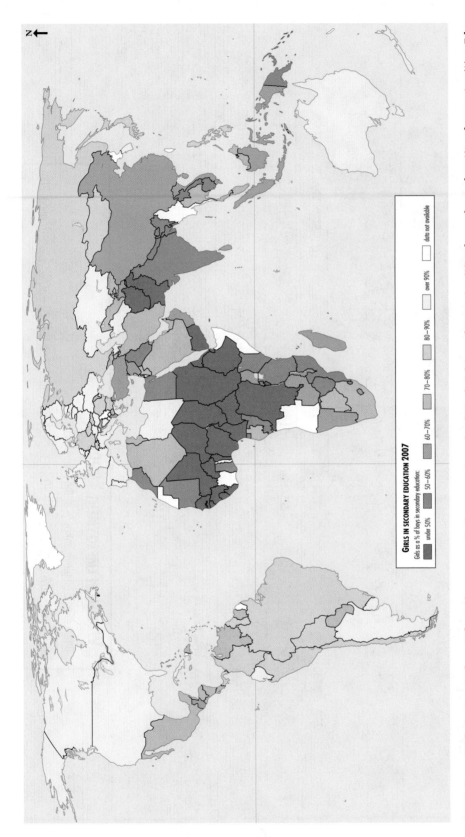

MAP 6.24 **Girls in Secondary Education 2007.** Both economic and political rights and opportunities depend on educational opportunities. Educating women has proven an excellent path towards economic development.

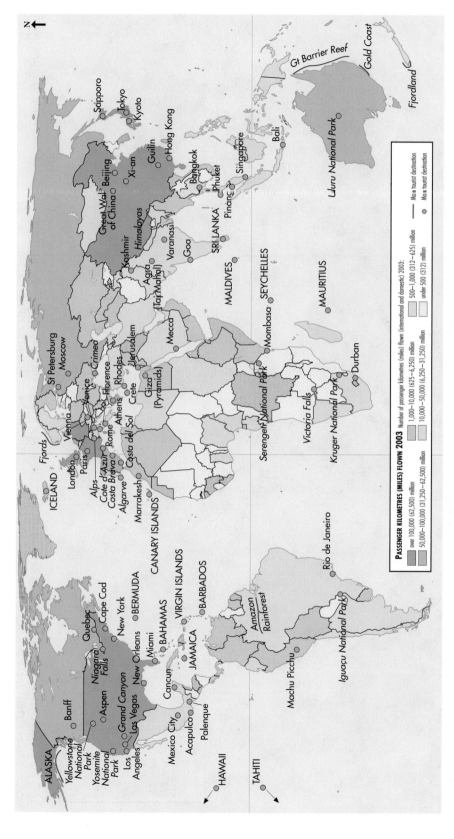

MAP 6.25 **Passenger Miles Flown 2003.** Contemporary globalization is marked by rapid transport and the commodification of culture in the form of tourism, the world's biggest industry.

PASSENGER KILOMETRES (MILES) FLOWN 2003 Number of passenger kilometres (miles) flown (international and domestic) 2003:

- over 100,000 (62,500) million
- 50,000–100,000 (31,250–62,500) million
- 10,000–50,000 (6,250–31,250) million
- 1,000–10,000 (625–6,250) million
- 500–1,000 (312–625) million
- under 500 (312) million

— Main tourist destination
○ Minor tourist destination

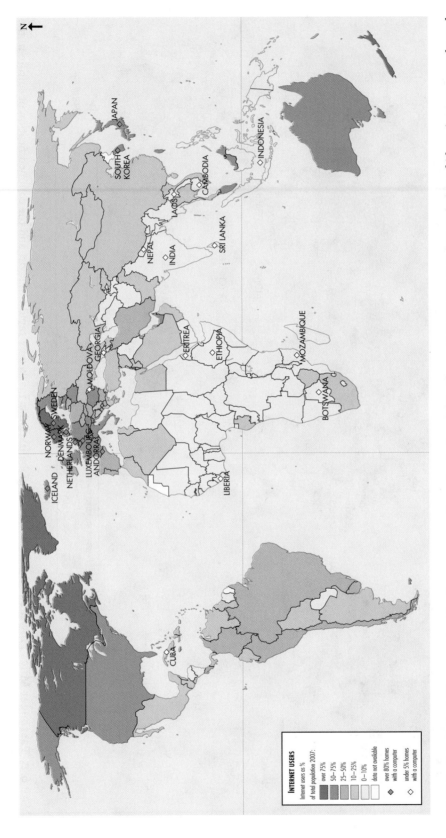

MAP 6.26 **Internet Users 2007.** Finally, even more than physical mobility, the near-instantaneous transmission of ideas, images, sounds, and services across virtual space has drawn the global community together into one changing world.

Geography Exercises

Prepared by Candace R. Gregory, Sacramento State University

Chapter 14

On Map 14.3, label the following cities. For each city, identify one of the following trade items that was likely to have passed through its markets.

Cities:
Mogadishu
Gede
Malindi
Zanzibar
Kilwa
Sofala
Great Zimbabwe
Cambay
Calicut
Aden

Trade Items:
Gold
Ivory
Slaves
Copper
Beads
Textiles
Sugar
Glass

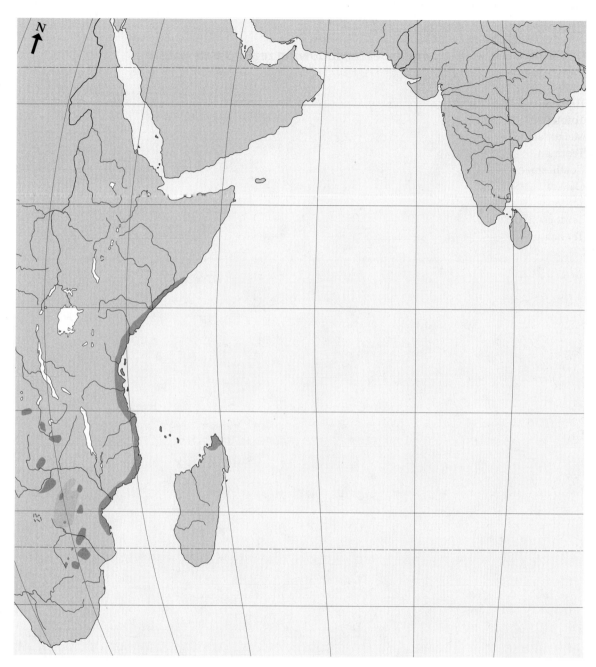

MAP 14.3 **The Swahili City-States, ca.** 1400

Chapter 15

Using Map 15.3, identify and label the following regions and states.

Tarasco
Yopitzinco
Tototepec
Metztitlan
Teotitlan
Coatlicamac
Oaxaca
Tlacopan
Texcoco
Tenochtitlán

N ←

MAP 15.3 **The Aztec Empire, ca.** 1520

Chapter 16

Using Map 16.2, and different color pencils, draw in the Ottoman conquests and expansions to the empire for the following dates.

1307 lands
1307 – 1481
1481 – 1520
1520 – 1566
1566 – 1683

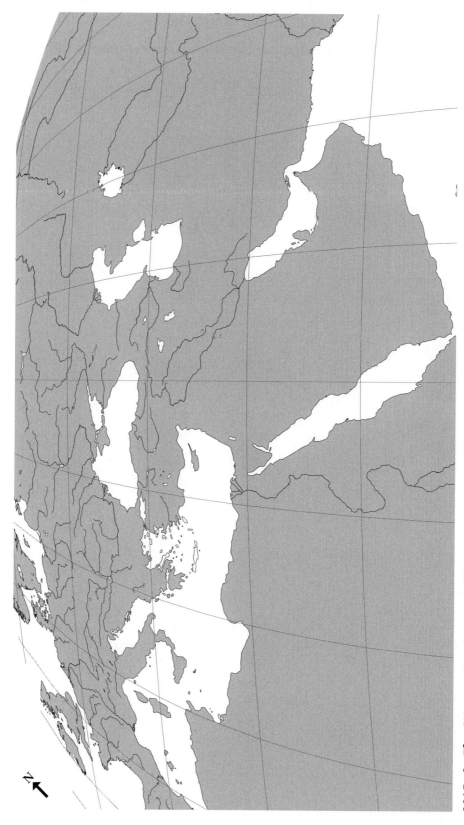

MAP 16.3 **The Ottoman Empire, 1307–1683**

Chapter 17

Using Map 17.2, label the following European states and provinces, c. 1580.

Portugal
Spain
Navarre
France
Alsace
Savoy
Austria
Bavaria
Saxony
Brandenburg
Mecklenburg
Spanish Netherlands
United Provinces
Pomerania
England
Ireland
Scotland
Italy
Ottoman Empire
Hungary
Bohemia
Poland-Lithuania
Russia
Norway
Sweden
Finland

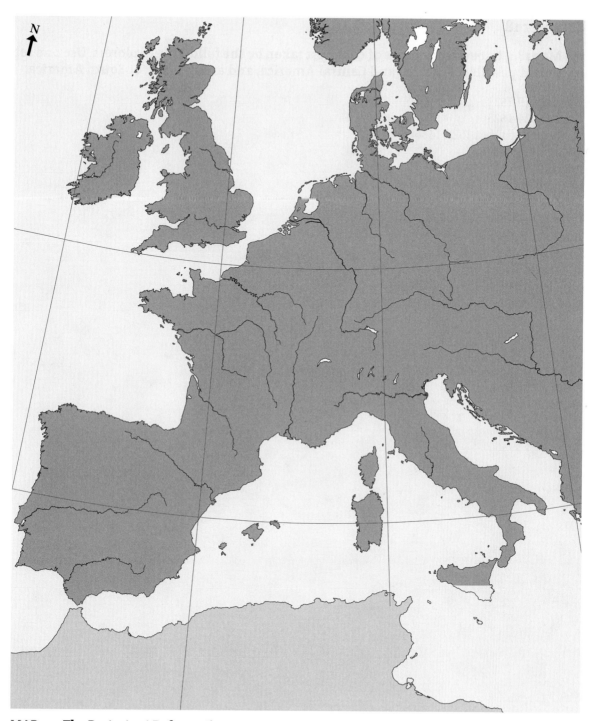

MAP 17.2 **The Protestant Reformation, ca.** 1580

Chapter 18

On Map 18.1, trace out the paths of conquest taken by the following explorers. Use one set of colored pencils for Mexico and Central America, and another set for South America.

Cortés 1519-1521
Cortés 1524-1525
Narváez and da Vaca 1528-1536
De Soto 1539-1545
Alarcon 1540
Coronado 1540-1542
Cabot 1526
Francisco Pizarro 1531-1533
Amalgro 1535-1537
Federmann 1537-1539
Benalcazar 1538-1539
Orrellana 1540
Gonzalo Pizarro 1540-1542
Valdivia 1540-1547
Quesada 1542

MAP 18.1 **The European Exploration of the Americas, 1519-1542**

Chapter 19

Using Map 19.1, and different colored pencils, draw in the borders of the following states and color in the areas occupied by the following peoples.

States:
Ethiopia
Mali
Songhay
Benin
Kongo

Peoples:
Fulani
Funj
Fur
Shilluk
Hausa

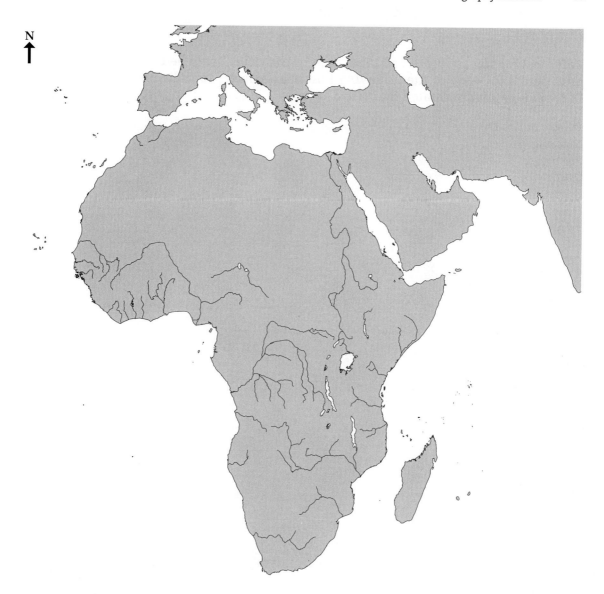

MAP 19.1 **Peoples and Kingdoms in Sub-Saharan Africa, 1450-1750**

Chapter 20

Refer to Map 20.5 to locate and label each of the cities listed below. Use a different colored pencil for each of the following European powers to indicate for each city what European power dominated that city c. 1650.

European Powers:
Netherlands
Portugal
Spain
Britain
Denmark
France

Cities:
Ahmadabad
Diu
Surat
Daman
Bombay
Goa
Bhatkal
Cochin
Quilon
Negombo
Colombo
Galle
Jaffra
Pondicherry
Madras
Masulipatam
Hugli
Calcutta
Serampore
Syriam
Ayutthaya
Kupang
Patani
Melaha
Johore
Pedang
Batavia
Palembang
Sambas
Sukadana
Makasar
Nagasaki

MAP 20.5 **European Trading Ports in the Indian Ocean, ca.** 1650

Chapter 21

Label the following regions, rivers, and cities on Map 21.4.

Regions:
Manchuria
Mongolia
Xinjiang
Tibet
Russia
Japan
Taiwan

Rivers:
Amur
Yellow
Yangzi

Cities:
Urmuchi
Beijing
Kaifeng
Xi'an
Nanjing
Hangzhou
Fuzhou
Guangzhou
Macao
Lhasa

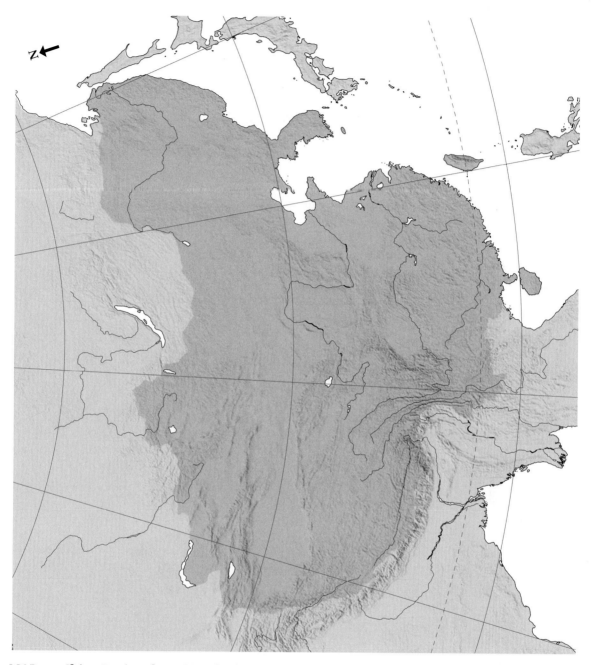

MAP 21.4 **China During the Reign of Qianlong**

Chapter 22

On Map 22.3, label the following nations created or recognized by the Congress of Vienna in 1815.

Spain
United Kingdom
France
Kingdom of Sardinia
Papal States
Kingdom of the Two Sicilies
Netherlands
Belgium
Denmark
Prussia
Austrian Empire
Ottoman Empire
Russia

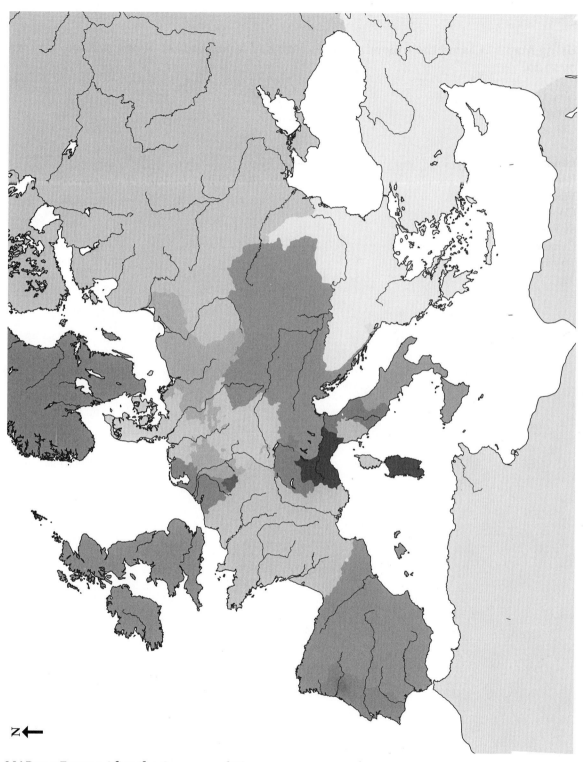

MAP 22.3 **Europe After the Congress of Vienna**

Chapter 23

Using Map 23.3, label the following cities that had a population of one million or more by 1900.

New York
Philadelphia
Chicago
Paris
London
Berlin
Vienna
Constantinople
St. Petersburg
Calcutta
Tokyo

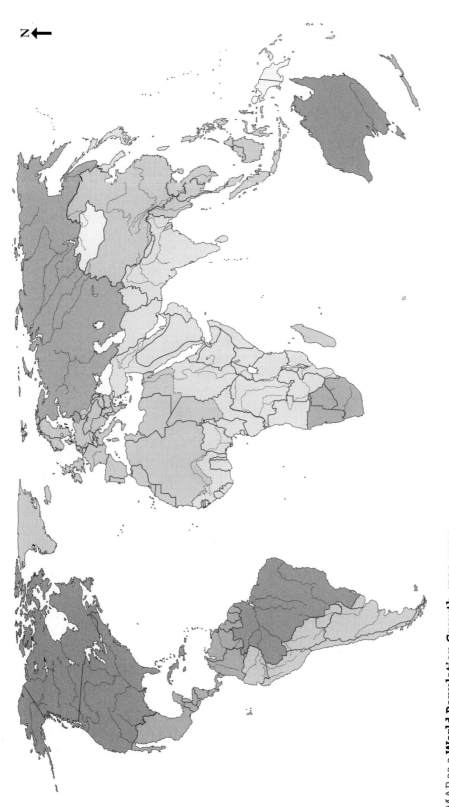

MAP 23.3 **World Population Growth, 1700–1900**

Chapter 24

On Map 24.2, label each of the following treaty ports in China, using six different color pencils or six different symbols for each of the foreign powers that dominated the treaty port.

Foreign Powers:

Britain
France
Germany
Japan
Portugal
United States

Treaty Ports:

Niuzhuang
Tianjin
Lüshun
Dalian
Dandong
Qingdao
Yantai
Chongqing
Wanxian
Yichang
Hankou
Nanjing
Shashi
Changshu
Jiujiang
Wuhu
Hangzhou
Zhenjiang
Suzhou
Shanghai
Ningbo
Wenzhou
Fuzhou
Amoy
Shantou
Sanshui
Guangzhou
Hong Kong
Macao
Zhanjiang
Haikou
Jiangmen
Wuzhou
Beihai
Nanning
Longzhou
Mengzi
Simao
Tengchong

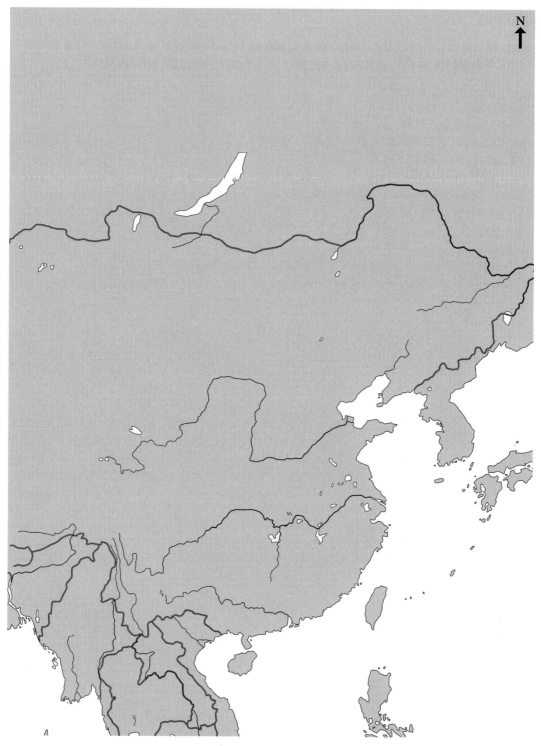

MAP 24.2 **Treaty Ports and Foreign Spheres of Influence in China, 1842-1907**

Chapter 25

For each of the following treaties, use a different color pencil and label Map 25.1 to indicate which regions of the Ottoman Empire were lost through which treaty.

Treaty of Karlowitz, 1683-1699
Treaty of Passarowitz, 1700-1718
Treaty of Kuchuk-Kainarji, 1719-1774
Treaty of Bucharest, 1775-1812
Treaty of Adrianople, 1813-1830
Treaty of Berlin, 1830-1878
Treaties of London and Bucharest, 1879-1915
Treaty of Lausanne, 1916-1923

MAP 25.1 **The Decline of the Ottoman Empire, 1683-1923**

Chapter 26

On Map 26.2, label the following regions. Use three different color pencils to identify which regions became British possessions before 1858, which were acquired by Britain after 1858, and which were dependent states.

Ceylon
Madras
Travancore
Mysore
Hyderbad
Central Provinces
Bastar
Orissa
Chota Nagpur
Gujarat
Sind
Rajputana
Baluchistan
Punjab
Kashmir
Oudh
Bihar
Bengal
Assam
Burma
Lower Burma
Pegu

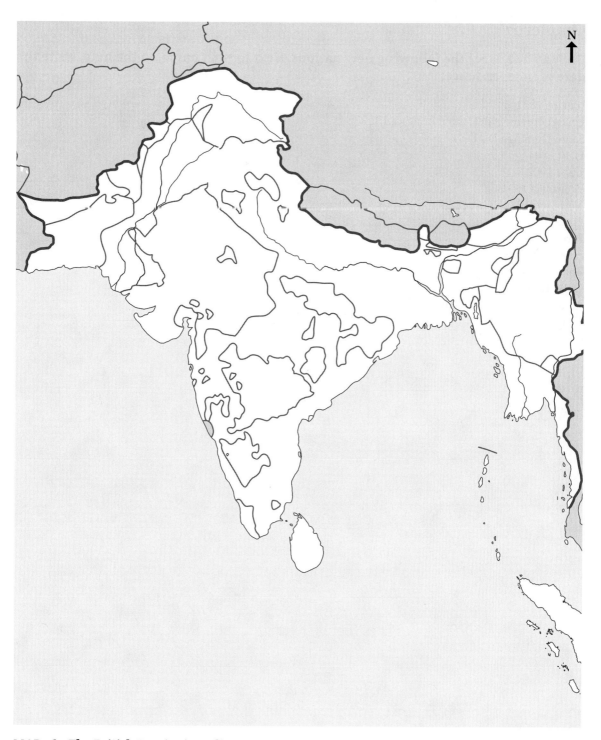

MAP 26.2 **The British Empire in India, 1858-1914**

Chapter 27

On Map 27.2, label the following new nations. Next to each name on the map, write the date of independence.

Mexico 1821
United Provinces of Central America 1823
Santo Domingo 1821
Haiti 1804
Cuba 1902
Venezuela 1831
New Granada 1831
Ecuador 1831
Peru 1824
Empire of Brazil 1822
Bolivia 1824
Chile 1818
Argentine Federation 1816
Uruguay 1828

MAP 27.2 **The New Nation-States of Latin America, 1830**

Chapter 28

Using the information provided on Map 28.8, label the following states, islands, and cities.

USSR
Mongolia
Manchukuo
Japan
China
Burma
French Indochina
Borneo
Okinawa
Iwo Jima
Mariana Islands
Hawaii
Midway
Philippines
Tokyo
Vladivostok
Hiroshima
Nagasaki
Nanjing
Beijing
Xi'an
Singapore

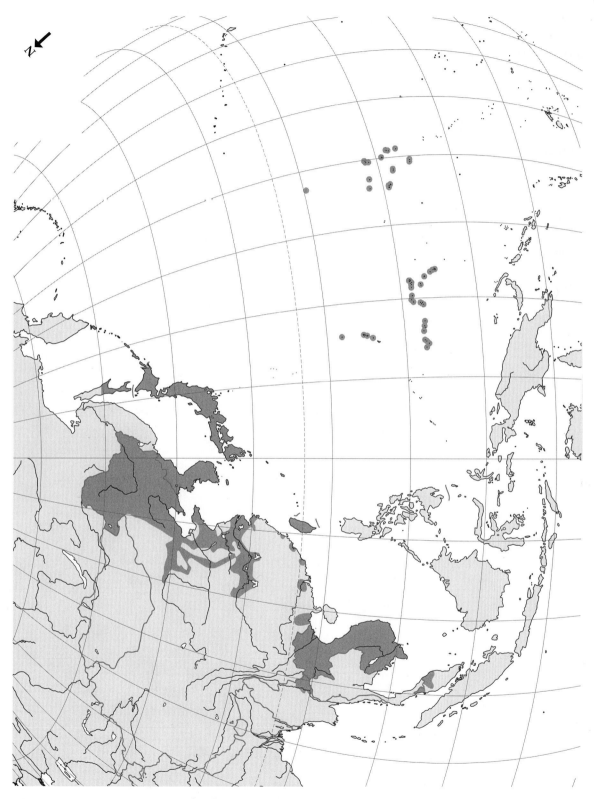

MAP 28.8 **World War II in the Pacific, 1937-1945**

Chapter 29

Using Map 29.3, label the following cities.

Guadalajara
Mexico City
San Salvador
Managua
Panama City
Barranquilla
Port-au-Prince
Caracas
Bogotá
Salvador
Lima-Callao
La Paz
Asuncion
Porto Alegre
Cordoba
Santiago

MAP 29.3 **Urbanization and Population Growth in Latin America and the Caribbean, ca.** 1950

Chapter 30

Using Map 30.2 indentify the fifteen republics that made up the Soviet Union.

Tajikistan
Kirghizstan
Turkmenistan
Uzbekistan
USSR
Georgia
Zimbabwe
Ukraine
Moldova
Belarus
Latvia
Lithuania
Estonia

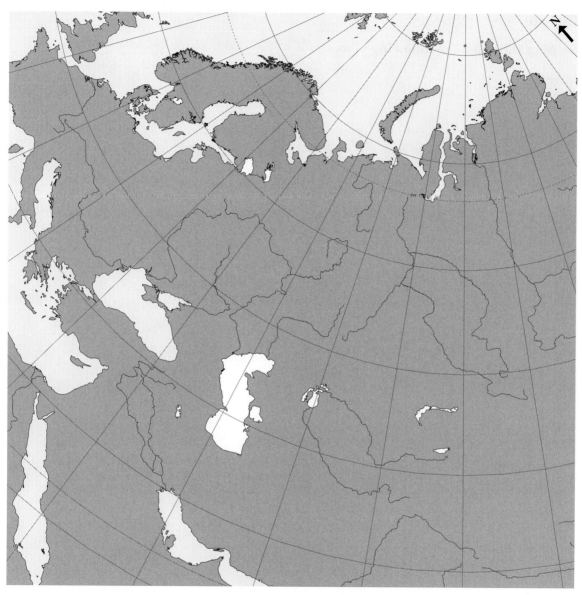

MAP 30.2 **The Fall of Communism in Eastern Europe and the Soviet Union**

Chapter 31

On Map 31.6, label the following places.

Morocco
Algeria
Tunisia
Libya
Egypt
South Sudan
Eritrea
Somalia
Ethiopia
Mauritania
Mali
Nigeria
Senegal
Democratic Republic of Congo
Rwanda

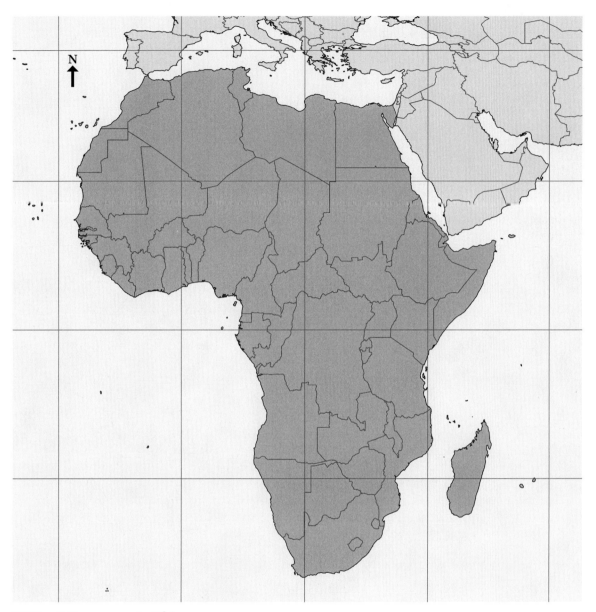

MAP 31.6 **Democracy in Africa, 1990-2011**

Concept Maps and Exercises

Exercises prepared by Robert Bond, San Diego Mesa Community College.

Chapter 15

1. How can we explain similarities in patterns of development in both the Americas and Eurasia?
2. What types of regional variations were there? Give examples.
3. How do these patterns compare when viewed on a timeline?
4. Using examples, compare the development of intensive agriculture, military states and empires, and temple-based city states in both the Americas and Eurasia.

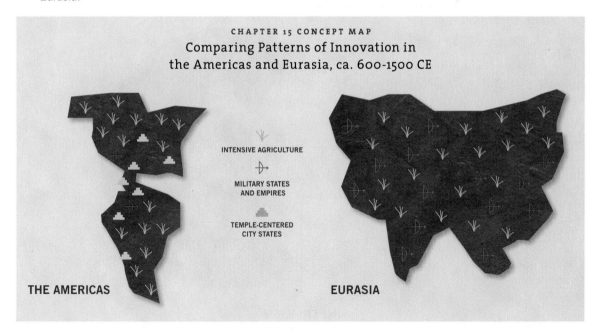

CHAPTER 15 CONCEPT MAP
Comparing Patterns of Innovation in
the Americas and Eurasia, ca. 600-1500 CE

INTENSIVE AGRICULTURE

MILITARY STATES
AND EMPIRES

TEMPLE-CENTERED
CITY STATES

THE AMERICAS

EURASIA

Chapter 16

1. What is a "fiscal-military" state? Does the Ottoman and Habsburg Empires both fit into that definition? Why?
2. What is "imperialism"? Were both empires "imperialistic"? Why?
3. In what ways did these empires project their power and grandeur?
4. Does this Concept Map change the way you think about the interactions between the Ottomans and the Habsburgs?

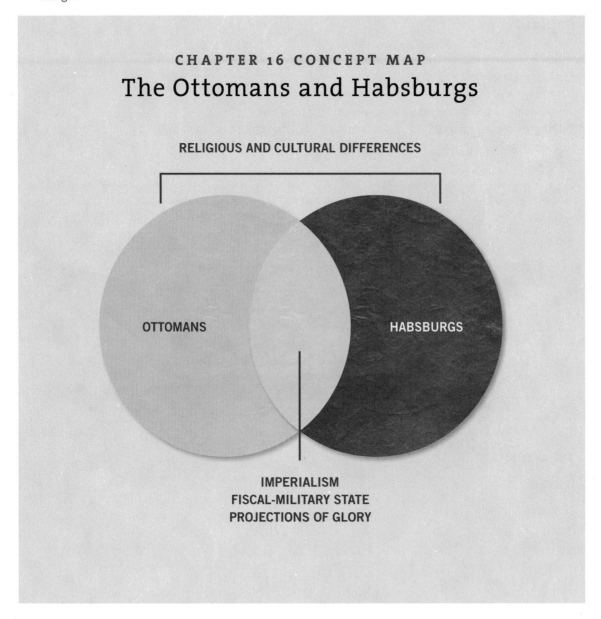

CHAPTER 16 CONCEPT MAP

The Ottomans and Habsburgs

RELIGIOUS AND CULTURAL DIFFERENCES

OTTOMANS

HABSBURGS

IMPERIALISM
FISCAL-MILITARY STATE
PROJECTIONS OF GLORY

Chapter 17

1. Examine the Concept Map closely. Why is each stage important to the development of the next stage?
2. Why is the mathematization of astronomy and physics perhaps the most important development?
3. What would have been the outcome if descriptive science had never been rendered obsolete?

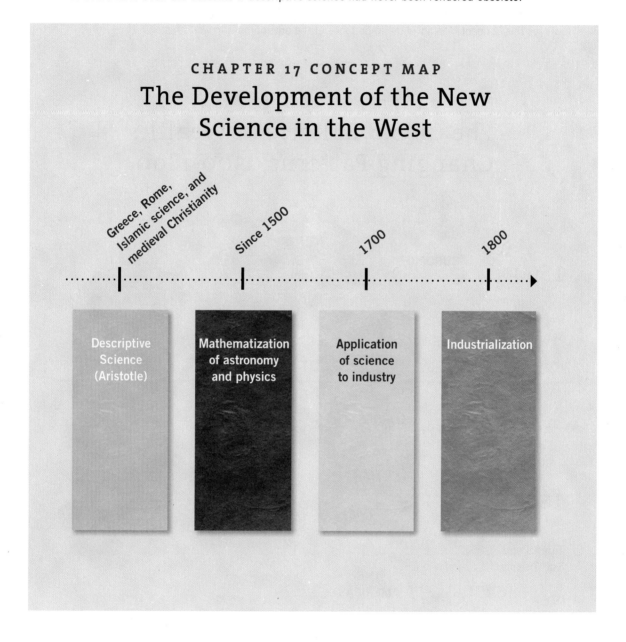

CHAPTER 17 CONCEPT MAP
The Development of the New Science in the West

Greece, Rome, Islamic science, and medieval Christianity

Since 1500

1700

1800

Descriptive Science (Aristotle)

Mathematization of astronomy and physics

Application of science to industry

Industrialization

Chapter 18

1. What is the major change that in the relationship between Europe and India and China that occurs between 1500 and 1800?
2. What does the change in the relative sizes of each region indicate? Why advantages did the American tropics and subtropics confer on Europe?
3. How does this Concept Map show the importance of the environment in world history?

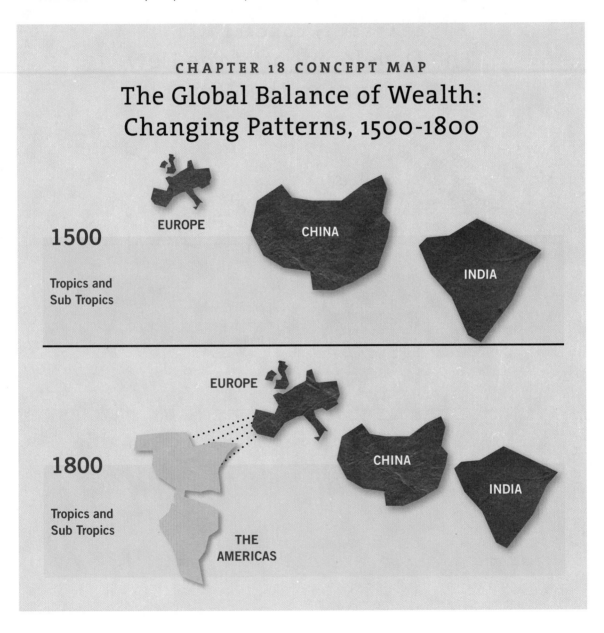

CHAPTER 18 CONCEPT MAP

The Global Balance of Wealth:
Changing Patterns, 1500-1800

Chapter 19

1. Examine the two ways of looking at the Atlantic World in this period.   What is revealed when one focuses on trade?   What dynamics are evident when looks at social and cultural patterns?
2. Can one fully appreciate African, European, and American history in this period without including both perspectives?

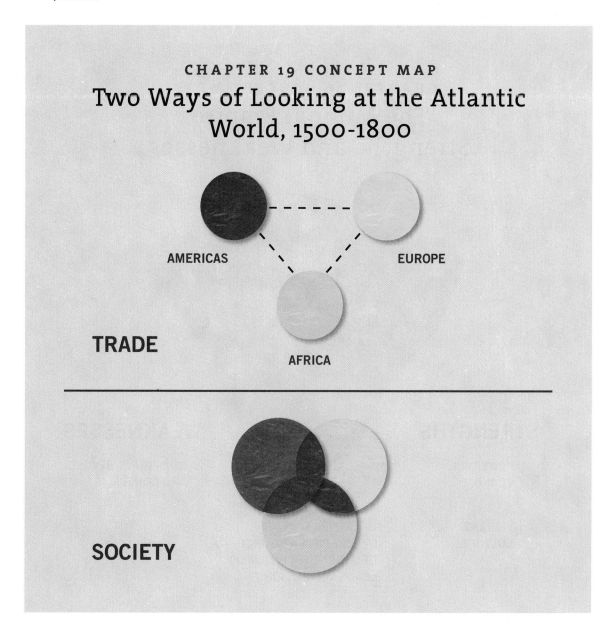

CHAPTER 19 CONCEPT MAP

Two Ways of Looking at the Atlantic World, 1500-1800

AMERICAS

EUROPE

TRADE

AFRICA

SOCIETY

Chapter 20

1. What were the sources of the strength of the Mughal economy? What role did geography play?
2. How did the Mughals contribute to Indian culture?
3. What syncretic religions emerged in India during the Mughal period? Why did they emerge?
4. What were the roots of conflict in the Mughal Empire? Were they only caused by religious differences between Muslim and Hindu?

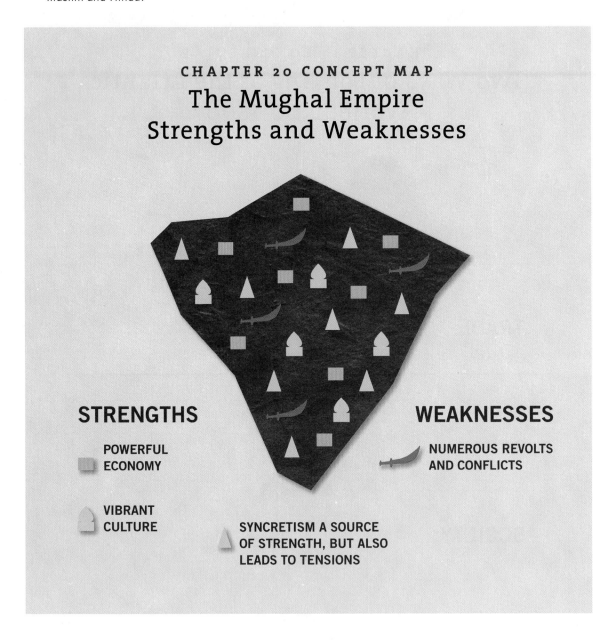

CHAPTER 20 CONCEPT MAP

The Mughal Empire
Strengths and Weaknesses

STRENGTHS

POWERFUL ECONOMY

VIBRANT CULTURE

SYNCRETISM A SOURCE OF STRENGTH, BUT ALSO LEADS TO TENSIONS

WEAKNESSES

NUMEROUS REVOLTS AND CONFLICTS

Chapter 21

1. Does the Concept Map reveal the differences in the "inner domains" of China and Japan?
2. Does the Concept Map reveal the different ways Japan and China controlled their "inner domains"?
3. How does the Concept Map show the different ways Japan and China regarded their "outer domains"?

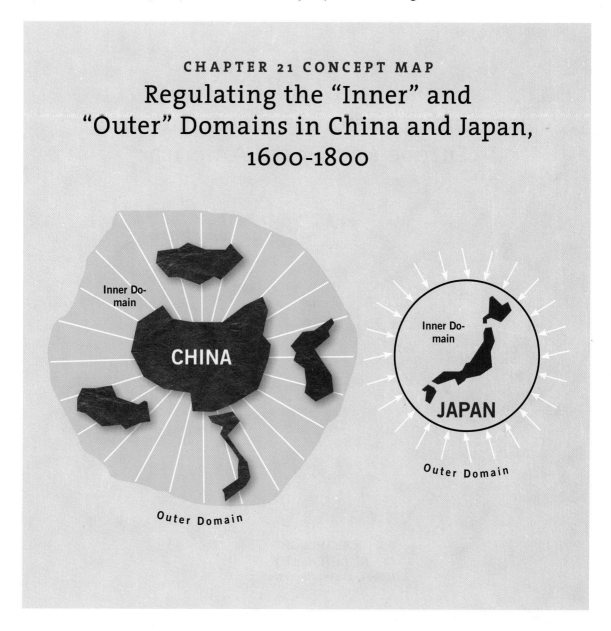

CHAPTER 21 CONCEPT MAP
Regulating the "Inner" and "Outer" Domains in China and Japan, 1600-1800

Chapter 22

1. How did Enlightenment political thought undermine divine-right monarchies?
2. What did Enlightenment political theorists contribute to the new political orders depicted on the right of the Concept Map?
3. What is ethnolinguistic nationalism? How do German and Italian unification reflect this specific type of nationalism? What are constitutional nation states?

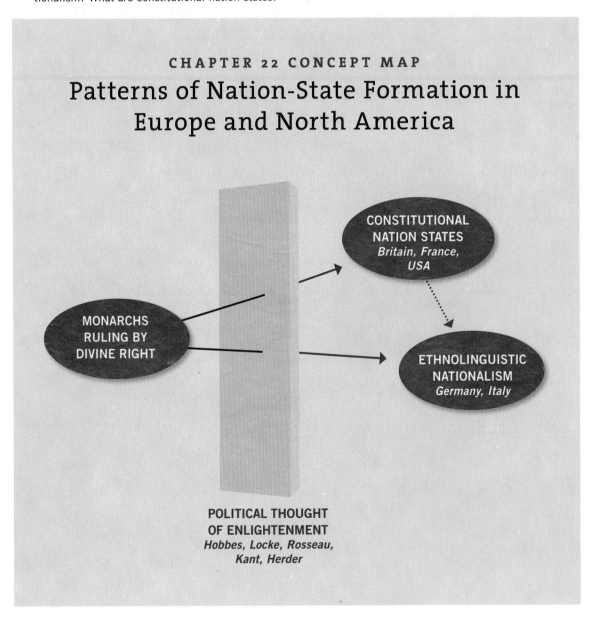

CHAPTER 22 CONCEPT MAP

Patterns of Nation-State Formation in Europe and North America

CONSTITUTIONAL
NATION STATES
Britain, France, USA

MONARCHS
RULING BY
DIVINE RIGHT

ETHNOLINGUISTIC
NATIONALISM
Germany, Italy

POLITICAL THOUGHT
OF ENLIGHTENMENT
Hobbes, Locke, Rosseau, Kant, Herder

Chapter 23

1. What are the differences between the first phase and the second phase of industrialization?
2. Why does the Concept Map get wider during the second phase?
3. Explain the relationship between industrialization and imperialism. Globalization? Social unrest? Migrant labor? Did these relationships change with time? with location?

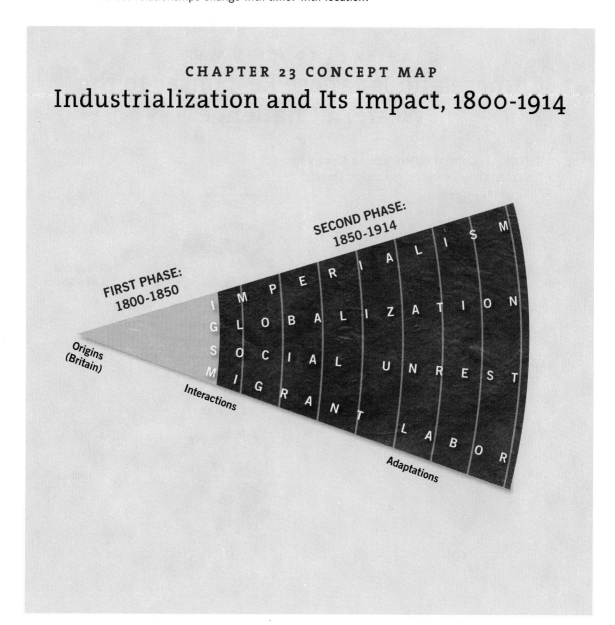

CHAPTER 23 CONCEPT MAP
Industrialization and Its Impact, 1800-1914

Chapter 24

1. In your own words discuss the two theories of Japanese and Chinese reactions to Western Imperialism as demonstrated in the Concept Map.
2. Which theory do you think has the most merit? Why? Can you provide evidence to back up your views?

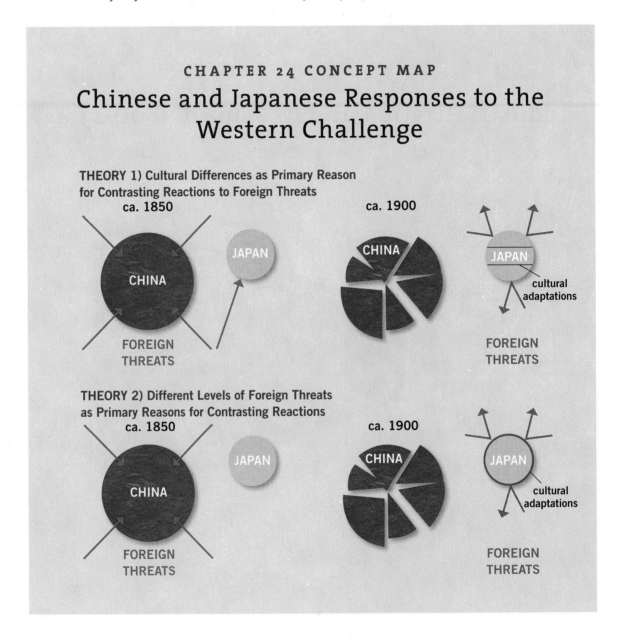

CHAPTER 24 CONCEPT MAP

Chinese and Japanese Responses to the Western Challenge

THEORY 1) Cultural Differences as Primary Reason for Contrasting Reactions to Foreign Threats

ca. 1850

ca. 1900

CHINA

JAPAN

CHINA

JAPAN

cultural adaptations

FOREIGN THREATS

FOREIGN THREATS

THEORY 2) Different Levels of Foreign Threats as Primary Reasons for Contrasting Reactions

ca. 1850

ca. 1900

CHINA

JAPAN

CHINA

JAPAN

cultural adaptations

FOREIGN THREATS

FOREIGN THREATS

Chapter 25

1. How does the Concept Map characterize the impact of industrialization on the Russian Empire? In the Ottoman Empire?

2. Why in the early twentieth century did ethnic nationalism appeal to many in the Ottoman Empire? Why did notions of pan-Slavism and revolutionary socialism appeal to certain groups in the Russian Empire?

3. How does the Concept Map show that each of these empire's transformations under the impact of modernity remained incomplete?

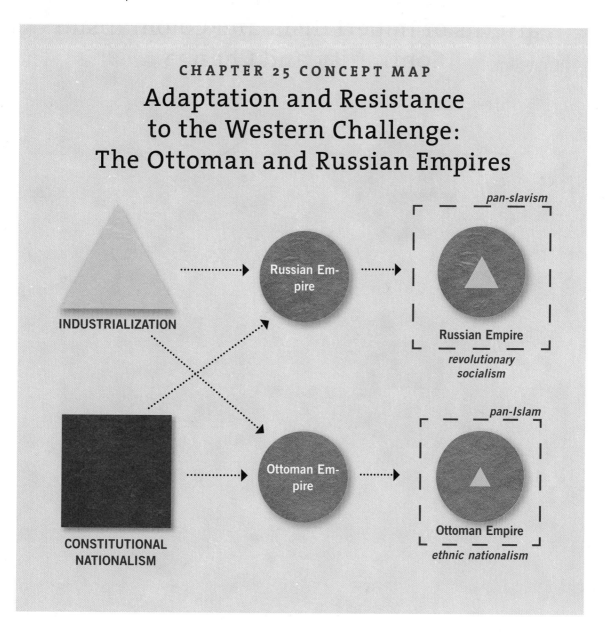

CHAPTER 25 CONCEPT MAP

Adaptation and Resistance to the Western Challenge: The Ottoman and Russian Empires

Chapter 26

1. What characterized European colonialism and imperialism before 1850? After 1850?
2. How did industrialization alter the nature of European expansion after 1850?

CHAPTER 26 CONCEPT MAP

Patterns of Imperialism and Colonialism: Continuity and Change

1) PRE 1850

Trade Forts

EMPIRE

2) POST 1850

Industrialization

EMPIRE

COLONIAL TERRITORIES

Chapter 27

1. Consider the two questions posed in the Concept Map. What do the chains in the older question represent? What do the red arrows in the new quester represent?
2. Thinking about the evidence presented in the chapter, which question is a better one to ask? Or are they both valid? How do the types of exports listed on the map contribute to either or both arguments?
3. Can these two questions be applied to other parts of the world during this period?

CHAPTER 27 CONCEPT MAP

Latin America in the Nineteenth Century

OLDER QUESTION: "Why did Latin America fail to industrialize?"

NEWER QUESTION: "Why did Latin America opt for export-led growth?"

USA

EUROPE

USA

EUROPE

SUGAR

SILVER

COFFEE

LIVESTOCK

BANANAS

GUANO AND NITRATES

Chapter 28

1. Review the patterns of constitutional nationalism, ethnolinguistic nationalism, and industrialization from previous chapters. How did these patterns, along with imperialism, contribute to the start of World War I?

2. How are national supremacism, capitalist democracy, and communism patterns of modernity? What role did World War I play in forging these patterns? What is the 19th-century antecedent for each of these patterns?

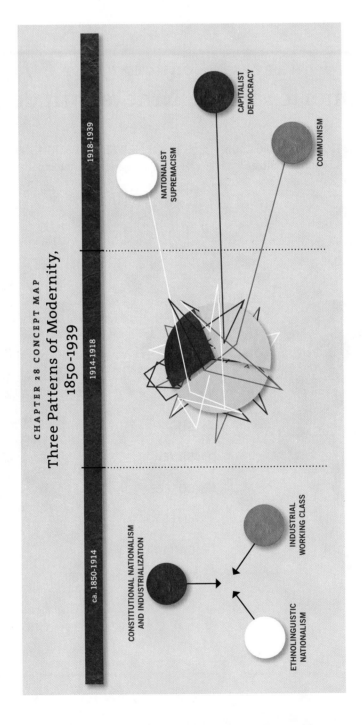

CHAPTER 28 CONCEPT MAP

Three Patterns of Modernity, 1850-1939

Chapter 29

1. What do you think accounts for the accelerating pace of change in the modern world?
2. How would you characterize change previous to 1850?
3. Why was the era of Global Imperialism so brief?

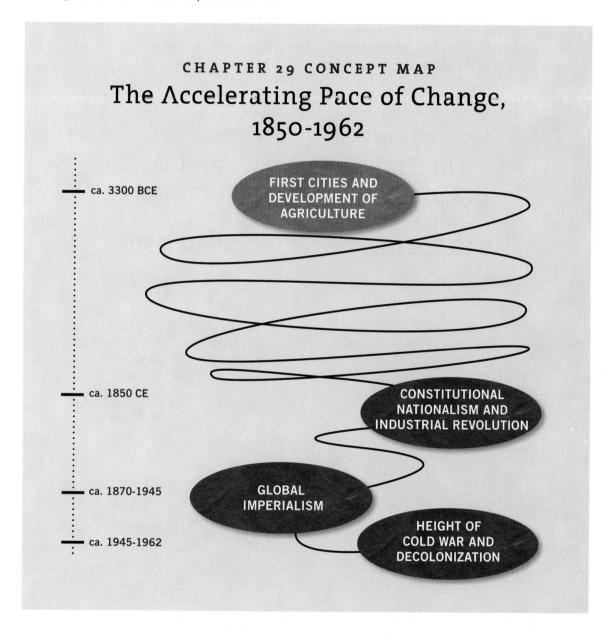

Chapter 30

1. What were the sources of conflict between capitalist democracies and communism? How was this conflict fought around the world?
2. Why was the non-aligned movement a third way?
3. Why caused the collapse of the Soviet Union and radical change in China's economy?
4. Do you think that the fall of communism marks "the end of history?"
5. What patterns do the Pac-Man symbols convey ?   Are the threats to the natural environment and the traditional values of society still serious concerns today?

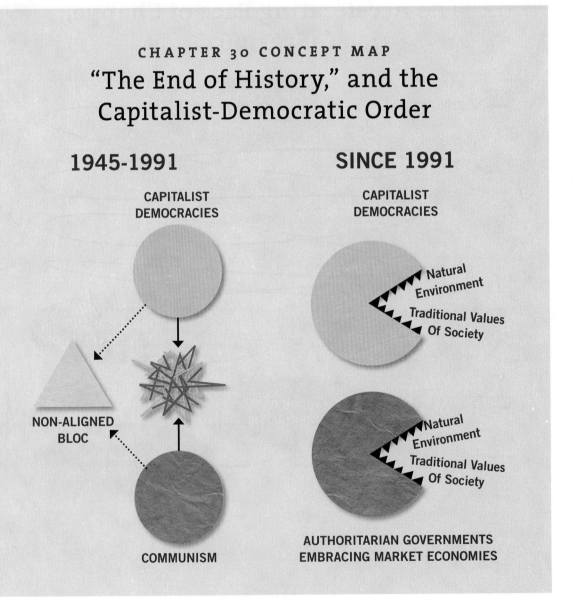

CHAPTER 30 CONCEPT MAP

"The End of History," and the Capitalist-Democratic Order

1945-1991

CAPITALIST DEMOCRACIES

NON-ALIGNED BLOC

COMMUNISM

SINCE 1991

CAPITALIST DEMOCRACIES

Natural Environment
Traditional Values Of Society

Natural Environment
Traditional Values Of Society

AUTHORITARIAN GOVERNMENTS EMBRACING MARKET ECONOMIES

Chapter 31

1. How does the Concept Map express the "devil's bargain of materialism" that haunts the modern world?
2. Is the interaction of population growth, technology, and affluence (materialism) a good formula for understanding the human impact on the planet?
3. What would a Concept Map that compares the world in 2012 with the world in 2022 look like?

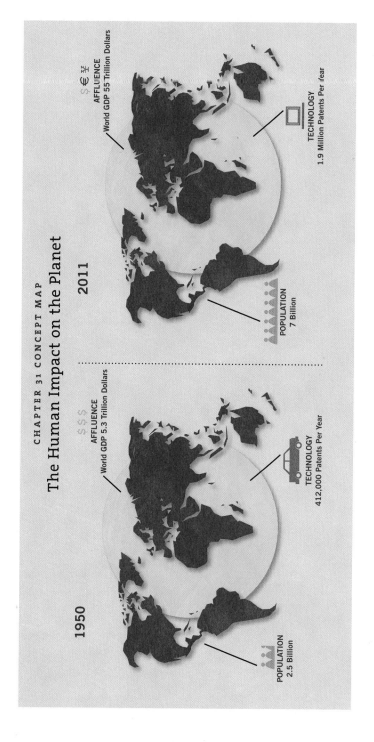

CHAPTER 31 CONCEPT MAP
The Human Impact on the Planet

2011

AFFLUENCE
World GDP 55 Trillion Dollars

TECHNOLOGY
1.9 Million Patents Per Year

POPULATION
7 Billion

1950

AFFLUENCE
World GDP 5.3 Trillion Dollars

TECHNOLOGY
412,000 Patents Per Year

POPULATION
2.5 Billion

NOTES

NOTES

NOTES

NOTES

Index